Techniques for Understanding Literature

A Handbook for Readers and Writers

Edward L. Hancock
University of Nevada at Reno

Wadsworth Publishing Company, Inc.
Belmont, California

© 1972 by Wadsworth Publishing Company, Inc., Belmont, California 94002. All rights reserved. No part of this book may be reproduced, stored in a retrieval system or transcribed, in any form or by any means, electronic, mechanical, photocopying, recording or otherwise, without the prior written permission of the publisher.

ISBN-0-534-00123-8
L. C. Cat. Card No. 75-180751
Printed in the United States of America

2 3 4 5 6 7 8 9 10—
76 75 74 73

Acknowledgments

The University of Chicago Press for excerpts from Richmond Lattimore, trans., *The Illiad*. © 1951 The University of Chicago Press.

Corinth Books for excerpts from LeRoi Jones, "Look for You Yesterday, Here You Come Today," in *Preface to a Twenty Volume Suicide Note*. © 1960 by LeRoi Jones.

Doubleday & Company, Inc. for excerpts from Clarence E. Mulford, "Hopalong Sits In," in *Great Tales of the American West;* and, for excerpts from J. U. Nicolson, trans., *Canterbury Tales*. Copyright, 1934, by Covici Friede, Inc.

Faber and Faber Ltd. for excerpts from T. S. Eliot, "The Waste Land," T. S. Eliot, "The Love Song of J. Alfred Prufrock," and T. S. Eliot, "The Hollow Men," in T. S. Eliot, *Complete Poems and Plays*.

Harcourt Brace Jovanovich, Inc. for excerpts from T. S. Eliot, "The Waste Land," T. S. Eliot, "The Love Song of J. Alfred Prufrock," and T. S. Eliot, "The Hollow Men," in *Collected Poems 1909–1962*.

Alfred A. Knopf, Inc. for excerpts from *The Short Stories of Katherine Mansfield*. © 1920, 1922, 1923, 1924, 1926, 1937 by Alfred A. Knopf, Inc.

The Macmillan Company for excerpts from "The Lake Isle of Innisfree" in *Collected Poems* by William Butler Yeats, Copyright 1906 by The Macmillan Company, renewed 1934 by William Butler Yeats; for excerpts from "Sailing to Byzantium" in *Collected Poems* by William Butler Yeats, Copyright 1928 by The Macmillan Company, renewed 1956 by Georgie Yeats; for excerpts from "The Second Coming" in *Collected Poems* by William Butler Yeats, Copyright 1924 by The Macmillan Company, renewed 1952 by Bertha Georgie Yeats; and, for excerpts from *The Modern Reader's Chaucer* by John S. P. Tatlock and Percy MacKaye, Copyright 1912 by The Macmillan Company, renewed 1940 by John S. P. Tatlock and Percy MacKaye. All reprinted with permission of The Macmillan Company.

Oxford University Press for excerpts from Leo Tolstoy, *War and Peace*, Louise and Aylmer Maude, trans.

The Society of Authors, on behalf of the Bernard Shaw Estate, for excerpts from Bernard Shaw, *Arms and the Man*.

A. P. Watt & Son for excerpts from William Butler Yeats, "The Lake Isle of Innisfree," William Butler Yeats, "Sailing to Byzantium," and William Butler Yeats, "The Second Coming" in *The Collected Poems of W. B. Yeats*. Reprinted by permission of Mr. M. B. Yeats and the Macmillan Co. of Canada.

Wesleyan University Press for excerpts from James Dickey, "The Fiend," in *Buckdancer's Choice*.

Preface

"Technique," it has been said, "is the means by which the writer's experience, which is his subject matter, compels him to attend to it; technique is the only means he has of discovering, exploring, developing his subject."[1] And from a reverse standpoint, technique is the reader's means of discovering the author's work, which is the reader's subject matter.

Both the quality of the papers written on literary works and the quality of discussions about them are, it seems to me, determined primarily by the quality of the reading that has preceded them. Reading techniques, rather than generalizations about how to read, bring the reader face to face with the work itself. This, then, is a practical handbook (one which the student may use on his own) that deals with specifics rather than generalities.

This handbook is not more "meaningful" or more "vital" than others in its field, but it may be more to the point. I have found that the use of specific techniques has the virtue of freeing the student from listening to talk about literature to making his own exploration of it.

Techniques may be of interest to different kinds of readers: the student wanting to understand more fully the story, poem, or drama given in his anthology; the composition student looking for ways to improve his own writing; the introduction-to-literature student acquainting himself with the process of critical analysis; the creative writer seeking insights into the handiwork of quality writers; the general reader of fiction desiring a fuller enjoyment of literature.

[1] Mark Schorer, "Technique as Discovery," *The Hudson Review*, Vol. I, No. 1, Spring 1948, p. 67.

Each of the nine chapters of this book defines one aspect of literary study, illustrates techniques for reading literature, and gives detailed suggestions for writing about it. Three sections following the nine chapters provide supplementary reading and writing suggestions. The first of these sections shows one way of preparing a critical paper on a literary work. The second section gives numerous writing exercises based on the passages of imaginative literature quoted in the chapters. Because imaginative literature is intense, concrete, and, in one sense, personal, it often provides both a model and a stimulus to the student writing about his own experience. The third section, a cross-reference chart, may be used by the student to test his comprehension of the various aspects of literary study discussed in each of the nine chapters and, also, to find theme topics of interest to him. Finally, there is a glossary and index of literary terms.

The examples used to illustrate the reading techniques and to define literary terms have been selected from a wide variety of fictional works. In "kind" they run the gamut from the expansive Russian novel to the brief lyric poem. In time and place they range from works written in the twentieth-century metropolis of New York to those written in the eighth century B.C. in ancient Greece. Classical authors such as Homer, Aeschylus, and Euripides are balanced with contemporary authors such as Lionel Trilling, Ralph Ellison, LeRoi Jones, and James Dickey. Shakespeare, Donne, Pope, Keats, Shaw, Yeats, Hemingway, Faulkner—authors seldom excluded from anthologies of literature—are included. A variety of recurrent literary themes have naturally been touched on: love, refined and metaphysical, in "A Valediction Forbidding Mourning"; hate, violent and vivid, in Flannery O'Connor's "Revelation." For the sake of tempo, the satiric lightness of *Candide* balances the emotional depths of *King Lear*. For a change of pace, a few uncommon selections have been included: Mulford's Hopalong Cassidy plays poker, Zane Grey's Tappan proposes love, and Wister's Virginian draws his steel.

Balance, tempo, and liveliness have been sought in addition to variety to produce a short handbook with little fat on it. Though there is an abundance of selections, the selections have been made, in every case, on the strength of their ability to illustrate specific reading techniques.

In the making of this book my first acknowledgment is to Walter Van Tilburg Clark, formerly of the University of Nevada, and to Walter Blair of the University of Chicago. From them I learned to "begin by taking [a work of literature] *absolutely*: that is to say, with mind intent on discovering just what the author's mind intended." The techniques used in this book reflect their influence.

I appreciate the help Mabel Brown, Robert Gorrell, Ace Remas, Rich Kuhn, Steve Rutter, and Ron Tyler gave me in preparing the manuscript. For her excellent typing I am grateful to Darleen Stringer, and for her fine editing to Dorothy Ohliger Conway. I thank Laura Hackett of the State University of New York, Stony Brook

Tom Massey of Chapman College, Gerald Messner of Cañada College, Jack Stevens of the University of Dubuque, and Robert H. Woodward of California State University, San Jose, for reading and commenting on the complete manuscript. And I wish especially to thank my wife, Sheila, for her sound judgment, stubborn criticism, and, more often than not, good humored assistance in the actual writing of the book.

Contents

Alphabetical List of Authors and Works
Introduction

1 Character   1

　　Round and Flat Characters—1;　Methods of Characterization—4;　Author's Comments—4;　Another Character's Comments—5;　Character's Comments on Himself—5 (Dialogue—5, Soliloquy—6, Dramatic Monologue—6);　Character's Actions—7.

Reading Techniques—8;　Marking Different Characters—9;　Listing Characteristics—9;　Diagramming a Dominant Characteristic—10.

Writing Suggestions—12.

2 Plot   14
　　The Multiple Plot—17;　The Modern Anti-Plot—18.

Reading Techniques—19　Outlining and Diagramming the Plot of Gradual Change—19;　Diagramming the Anti-Plot—21.

Writing Suggestions—23.

3 Setting   24
　　Functions of Setting—24:　Setting as It Causes Action—24;　Setting as It Affects Character—25; Setting as It Reveals Character—26;　Setting as Background—27;　Setting as a State of Mind—28.

Reading Techniques—29　Outlining and Marking to Distinguish Abstract Statements and Concrete Details—29;　Diagramming and Outlining to Discover Abstract Correlations of Setting—31.

Writing Suggestions—33.

4 Point of View 34
    Major Points of View in Narratives—35: Omniscient—35; Third-Person-Limited—37; First-Person—39; Stream of Consciousness—40.

Reading Techniques—41   Diagramming and Outlining Point of View—41.

Writing Suggestions—44.

5 Style 45
    Diction—46: Meaning—46 (Denotation—46, Connotation—46); Sound—47 (Alliteration—47, Assonance—48, Pun—48, Onomatopoeia—48); Syntax—49: The Loose Sentence—49; The Periodic Sentence—49; The Balanced Sentence—50.

Reading Techniques—51   Intense Logical Constructions—52; Unusual Syntactical Constructions—53.

Writing Suggestions—55.

6 Tone 57
    Meaning and Attitude—60: Explicit Meaning—60; Ironic Meaning—60 (Verbal Irony—60, Situational Irony—61, Cosmic Irony—62, Dramatic Irony—63).

Reading Techniques—64   Describing Diction to Discover Tone—64.

Writing Suggestions—65.

7 Imagery 67
    Types of Imagery—67: Literal Images—67; Figures of Speech—68 (Simile—68, Metaphor—69, Personification—69, Overstatement—69, Understatement—70); Complex Imagery—70.

Reading Techniques—72; Drawing—72; Listing—73; Marking—75.

Writing Suggestions—77.

8 Symbolism 79
    Emphasis and Symbolism—80; Discovering and Interpreting Symbols—82: A Word as a Symbol

—82;   A Figure of Speech as a Symbol—83; An Event as a Symbol—84;   The Total Action as a Symbol—85;   Allegory—87.

Reading Techniques—88   Diagramming and Listing Concrete Details Embodying the Abstract Idea of a Work—88.

Writing Suggestions—91.

9 Structure   93
Kinds of Structure—94:   Thematic Structure—94; Logical Structure—97;   Emotional Structure—98.

Reading Techniques: Outlining the Relationship of Parts—100.

Writing Suggestions—103.

Theme, Thesis, and the Writing of a Critical Paper   105
Two Definitions of Theme—105;   A Definition of Thesis—105;   Preparing a Critical Paper—106 (Limiting the Topic—106, Formulating a Thesis Statement—106, Outlining Support for the Thesis Statement—107).

Writing Exercises   109

Selected Analytic Cross Reference Chart   114

Glossary and Index of Literary Terms   116

Index   131

Alphabetical List of Authors of Works Used as Examples

Aeschylus *Agamemnon*   63
Anonymous *Beowulf*   70
—————— "Frankie and Johnny"   14-17
Matthew Arnold "Dover Beach"   73
Jane Austen *Pride and Prejudice*   9
Honoré de Balzac *Père Goriot*   29-31
Robert Browning "Caliban upon Setebos"   6-7
John Bunyan *The Pilgrim's Progress*   88
Joyce Cary *The Horse's Mouth*   26-27
Geoffrey Chaucer *The Canterbury Tales*   45-46, 58-59
Anton Chekhov "In the Cart"   21-23
Joseph Conrad *The Heart of Darkness*   41-43, 71-72
Daniel Defoe *The Adventures of Robinson Crusoe*   49
Charles Dickens *Bleak House*   82-83
—————— *Hard Times*   1-3
James Dickey "The Fiend"   80-82
John Donne "The Canonization"   69
—————— "A Valediction Forbidding Mourning"   75-77
Fydor Dostoyevsky *Crime and Punishment*   4-5
—————— *The Possessed*   80
Lawrence Durrell *The Alexandria Quartet*   25-26
T. S. Eliot "The Hollow Men"   69
—————— "The Love Song of J. Alfred Prufrock"   71
—————— *The Waste Land*   58-59
Ralph Ellison *The Invisible Man*   61-62
Euripides *The Trojan Women*   27-28
William Faulkner "A Rose for Emily"   31-33, 64-65
E. M. Forster *Howards End*   81-82
Johann Wolfgang von Goethe *Faust*   83-84
Zane Grey *Tappan's Burro*   5-6
Thomas Hardy *Jude the Obscure*   62
Nathaniel Hawthorne "Young Goodman Brown"   19-21
Ernest Hemingway *A Farewell to Arms*   81-82
—————— *The Sun Also Rises*   67-68
George Herbert "The Collar"   47
—————— "Virtue"   93-94
Homer *The Iliad*   10-12

————— *The Odyssey*   24-25
Henry James   "The Beast in the Jungle"   100-103
—————   "The Real Thing"   49-50
LeRoi Jones   "Look for You Yesterday, Here You Come Today"   68
James Joyce   *Ulysses*   18, 40-41
—————   *Finnegans Wake*   47-48
Franz Kafka   "The Hunger Artist"   85-87
John Keats   "Ode to a Nightingale"   73-74
Katherine Mansfield   "Bliss"   37-39, 106-108
—————   "The Fly"   18
Andrew Marvell   "To His Coy Mistress"   97-98
John Milton   "L'Allegro"   69
Clarence E. Mulford   "Hopalong Sits In"   9-10
Frank Norris   *McTeague*   88-91
Flannery O'Connor   "Revelation"   7-8
Plato   *The Republic*   87
Alexander Pope   *An Essay on Man*   50-51
William Shakespeare   *Hamlet*   51-53, 60-61
—————   *King Lear*   2-3
—————   *Midsummer Night's Dream*   17-18
—————   *Richard III*   6
—————   *The Tempest*   53-55
George Bernard Shaw   *Arms and the Man*   94-97
Leo Tolstoy   *War and Peace*   35-37
Lionel Trilling   "Of This Time, Of That Place"   79-80
Mark Twain (Samuel L. Clemens)   *The Adventures of Huckleberry Finn*   39-40
François-Marie Arouet de Voltaire   *Candide*   3-4
Owen Wister   *The Virginian*   57-58
William Wordsworth   "The World Is Too Much With Us"   60
William Butler Yeats   "The Lake Isle of Innisfree"   34
—————   "Sailing to Byzantium"   28-29
—————   "The Second Coming"   98-100

Introduction to the Reader

You need not begin at the beginning of *Techniques*. Each chapter is a unit in itself, and you may start with any chapter. The first three chapters—character, plot, setting—will acquaint you with the basics of most literary works. The last six chapters deal with progressively more subtle and, perhaps, more sophisticated aspects of literature. Your interest and the nature of the work you are studying can determine which chapter you will use. With one work you may find it useful to begin with a study of plot; with another, tone; with another, structure; and with still another, the interrelation of all three. The more reading techniques you are able to employ and the more connections you are able to make between parts of a work, the fuller your reading will be.

It may not, of course, be sensible to read everything in as great detail as is suggested in this book. But if you are making a special study of a poem, or if you simply want to understand a short story more, you may find that the techniques suggested here help.

Action synopses and quoted passages from complete works should give you sufficient information for understanding the techniques. Since it is the *technique* itself that you are learning, you need not have read the whole work to understand its use. Passages from complex works of literature have been used to illustrate some of the techniques. If you understand a technique when it is applied to what is considered a masterpiece, you should have little difficulty applying it to less intense literature.

Each chapter is divided into three parts: (1) **Explanation,** (2) **Reading Techniques,** (3) **Writing Suggestions.** The explanations define, mainly by example, the particular phase of literary study considered in the chapter. The reading techniques illustrate—with markings, drawings, outlines, and diagrams

—specific reading methods. The writing suggestions provide clues for writing a critical paper.

The book concludes with three sections that are designed to help you write: **Theme, Thesis, and the Writing of a Critical Paper** shows one way of preparing an analytical paper on a literary work; **Writing Exercises** suggests topics for compositions based on your own experience; and an **Analytical Cross-Reference Chart** indicates theme topics which may be of special interest to you. Following these three sections is **A Glossary and Index of Literary Terms.**

Reading literature and writing about it may be both enchantment and discipline—you may find that techniques can nourish both.

Character

1

CHARACTER refers both to the people in a work of literature and to the characteristics of those people. The reader must know not only who the characters are in a literary work but also their distinctive qualities, both physical and psychological.

Round and Flat Characters

One way of beginning to understand character is to distinguish between flat and round characters.[1] A **FLAT character,** like Charles Dickens's Josiah Bounderby in *Hard Times,* **dramatizes a single idea.** In effect, Dickens is saying, "Here is a man who bases himself solely on the assumption that he is a self-made man." Every time Bounderby appears in the novel, what he says illustrates this assumption. Josiah Bounderby of Coketown—"rich man: banker, merchant . . . could never sufficiently vaunt himself a self-made man":

> I haven't always occupied my present situation of life . . .
>
> I was born in a ditch . . . a foot of water in it . . .
>
> I was born with inflammation of the lungs . . .
>
> I was so ragged and dirty that you wouldn't have touched me with a pair of tongs . . .
>
> I was born in a ditch, and my mother ran away from me . . .

[1] See E. M. Forster, *Aspects of the Novel* (New York: Harcourt, Brace, 1927), pp. 103ff.

> I was determined ... to pull through ...
>
> ... there's no imaginative sentimental humbug about me.

There is little more to Bounderby than the "sonorous repetitions" of his boasts.

By contrast, William Shakespeare's dramatic figure King Lear is **ROUND**; that is, he **reveals the complexities of a man whose actions are the outgrowth of the many facets of his nature.**

The play opens in Lear's palace, with the old king eighty years "and upwards" in the act of giving his kingdom to his three daughters upon the requirement that each profess the love she feels for him.

> Tell me, my daughters, ...
> Which of you shall we say doth love us most?
> That we our largest bounty may extend ...

Two contradictory sides of Lear's character are immediately apparent: out of generosity and love he will give his daughters all; out of vanity he requires their obedience and adulation before he gives it.

The eldest daughters, Goneril and Regan, tell the old king the extravagant lies he wants to hear. But the youngest daughter, Cordelia, refuses to use "the glib and oily art" of flattery to gratify her father's vanity. "I love your majesty/according to my bond; nor more nor less." Lear reacts: "Better thou/Hadst not been born than not t'have pleased me better." Another side of Lear's character leaps to the surface, a deep-seated egoism that overrides his love. Childishly and fitfully he responds to Cordelia's abrupt but honest expression of her love.

Lear casts out Cordelia, the daughter he most loves and who most loves him, and divides his kingdom between the two flatterers. Once they have everything, Goneril and Regan treat their dependent father not with the love and gratitude he demands but with indignities. They insult him to his face and deny him food and shelter. Insane rage at this injustice drives Lear out into a stormy night. He confronts the elements, correlatives of his emotional state.

> Rumble thy bellyful! Spit, fire! spout, rain!
> Nor rain, wind, thunder, fire, are my daughters:
> I tax not you, you elements, with unkindness;
> ...
> But yet I call you servile ministers,
> That have with two pernicious daughters join'd
> Your high engender'd battles 'gainst a head
> So old and white as this. O! O! 'tis foul!

The complexities of Lear's character multiply. So great is his fury that it contends with the storm's. In his mind, fixed on the injustice done him, the elements seem to be in league with his two daughters. The strength, the force, the outraged vanity of Lear's character take on cosmic proportions.

After suffering violently from the storm of anger that rages within him and the bitterness of the storm that beats down on him from without, Lear recognizes that his Fool, who has accompanied him into the storm, suffers from the cold, and Lear bids him take shelter in a hovel.

> In, boy; go first. You houseless poverty,—
> Nay, get thee in. I'll pray, and then I'll sleep.
>
> [*Fool goes in.*]
>
> Poor naked wretches, wheresoe'er you are,
> That bide the pelting of this pitiless storm,
> How shall your houseless heads and unfed sides,
> Your loop'd and window'd raggedness, defend you
> From seasons such as these? O, I have ta'en
> Too little care of this!

Another side of Lear emerges. Recognition of the pain his Fool is suffering, pity for him, and compassionate understanding of the misery of the world's "poor naked wretches" have replaced Lear's unbridled rage. He is now capable of remorse and prayer.

At the end of the play, between two violently passionate outbursts (one of despair, the other of an ecstasy that breaks his heart) Lear, "the great rage . . . kill'd in him," says to one attendant upon the scene, "Pray you, undo this button . . ." The button is undone and Lear says, "thank you, sir."

Lear's being could be illustrated only through an exposition of the many different facets of his character as they have determined and have grown out of the events he experiences. "Upon the rack of this tough world" this "foolish, fond" old man, by way of the flaws and strengths of his character, is brought to this tragic end—but not before he has achieved an emotional relation to life, a wisdom, a beauty of character he could not have had before his misfortunes and sufferings.

A round character like Lear is **DYNAMIC**; that is, **he is altered or modified by the events he experiences.** Though always believable, Lear's character is not always predictable, for he responds to his experiences in a number of different ways. **A flat character,** on the other hand, is **STATIC**; that is, he **is unchangeable and thus predictable, for there is only one side to him.** What will Josiah Bounderby of Coketown say? "I pulled through it, though nobody threw me a rope."

This is not to say that flat characters are unworthy of analysis, for they may illustrate the central idea of a work. Pangloss in Voltaire's *Candide* is an example of the use of a flat character as one of the main characters. "O, my dear Pangloss! The greatest of philosophers!" says his devoted pupil, the naïve Candide. Pangloss, who teaches "meta-physico-theologocosmolonigology" and is the "oracle" of Baron Thunder-ten-tronck's castle in Westphalia, observes "that noses were made to wear spectacles; and so we have spectacles"; is seen "in the bushes, giving a lesson in experimental physics to . . . a very pretty and docile brunette"; loses his position, becomes a beggar, receives "twenty strokes of the bull's pizzle"; is "hanged, dissected, stunned with blows and made to row in the galleys"; but continues to say that everything is for the best in this "best of all possible worlds."

Though all the happenings in the novel conspire to prove the contrary, Pangloss will proclaim every time he appears on the printed page, "This is the best of all possible worlds." Pangloss is a flat character and to attempt to analyze him as if he were round would be a mistake. He is there in the novel as an animated illustration of the blissful senselessness of an airily optimistic philosophy.

The distinction between flat and round characters is relative. The flatter a character, the simpler he is and the less he changes; the less he affects events or is affected by them. The rounder a character, the more complex he is and the more he changes; the more he affects events and is affected by them. If an author wishes the chief feature of a character to be outstanding, he may isolate it and show only that feature, in which case the character will be flat. If the author wishes to expose many features of a character, he will show the interaction of various aspects of the character's being, in which case the character will be round.

When you analyze a flat character, you will need to see his one trait, sum it up in a sentence, and realize how the idea he dramatizes functions within the whole work. When you analyze a round character, you will need to see the different traits of his personality and realize how they relate to other aspects of the total work.

Methods of Characterization

Acquaintance with the ways an author reveals a character provides the basis for character analysis. You will find clues to a character's personality in the different ways an author discloses character: (1) by telling the reader about him, (2) by letting one character tell about another character, (3) by presenting what the character says, (4) by showing the character in action.

Author's Comments

An author may explain the psychological make-up of a character. In Fyodor Dostoyevsky's *Crime and Punishment* the reader sees Katerina Ivanovna, the consumptive wife of the dissolute drunkard Semyon Zakharovich Marmelodov, drag her husband by the hair as he crawls drunkenly, submissively on his knees at her side. And yet Katerina is a sympathetic character. She is made so partly by the author's frequent references to her overwrought, nervous constitution.

> Katerina . . . was by nature of a humorous, cheerful, and peaceable disposition, but constant failure and unhappiness had brought her to the point of so *furiously* desiring and demanding that everybody should live in joy and harmony, and *should not dare* to live otherwise, that the slightest discord, the smallest setback, drove her at once almost to madness, and in an instant, from indulging the brightest hope and fancies, she would fall to cursing fate, smashing and destroying anything that came to hand, and banging her head against the wall.

When analyzing a character according to what the author says about him, you will need to remember that you cannot always explicitly believe what some authors say. Henry James, for example, frequently refers to his main character in "The Middle Years" as "poor" Dencombe. James is not (though the reader may not realize this until near the end of the story) simply commiserating with Dencombe but is saying more nearly, perhaps, "Poor, blind, disillusioned, misguided Dencombe; you poor fool, conceitedly misspending your life." The *tone* of the author's comments is the clue to his meaning.

Another Character's Comments

We, the readers, know Marmelodov in *Crime and Punishment* by what he has told us about himself—he has lain helplessly drunk while his wife was beaten by another man, has stolen his wife's savings, drunk her "very stockings," and has let his daughter sell herself in order to support the family. But we also know Marmelodov by Katerina's analysis of him.

After the drunken Marmelodov falls under the wheels of a carriage and dies, leaving his wife and children penniless, Katerina says:

> My late husband certainly had that weakness, and everybody knows it.... But he was a generous-hearted, good man, who loved and respected his family.... Just think ... they found a gingerbread cock in his pocket; he was dead drunk, but he had remembered his children.

By seeing Marmelodov through the eyes of his wife, the reader gains new insights into his character.

Often it is not sensible, of course, to believe what one character says about another. In Shakespeare's *Othello*, when Desdemona says "O good Iago" what she says tells us nothing about that "inhuman dog" Iago—unless we also take into account the character of the speaker—the innocent, loving Desdemona. And then our sense of Iago's ability to counterfeit becomes intensified by way of Desdemona's opinion of him.

Character's Comments on Himself

What a character says about something may reveal as much about him as it does about his subject. In **dialogue, soliloquy,** and **dramatic monologue** characters talk and the reader is given clues to their feelings, desires, and mental processes.

Dialogue   In a love scene from Zane Grey's story "Tappan's Burro" the words Tappan uses to express his love for Madge characterize him:

> "Madge, you mean take you away—and marry you?" he replied.
> "Oh, yes—yes—marry me, if you love me. ... you do, don't you?—Say you do."

"I reckon that's what ails me, Madge," he replied, simply.
"*Say* so, then," she burst out.
"All right, I do," said Tappan, with heavy breath. "Madge, words don't come easy for me. . . ."

Neither suave nor sophisticated, Tappan, a brawny prospector who favors "the lonely water holes," is more articulate with his burro, Jenet, than with Madge. What Tappan says emphasizes his nature—"a brooding, plodding fellow, not conscious of sentiment."

Soliloquy A soliloquy is **a speech given by a character when he is alone, revealing his private thoughts and emotions.** The character is thinking out loud to himself. What he says discloses essential information and provides the surest guide to his inner self. Here is Richard from Shakespeare's *Richard III*:

> But I, that am not shaped for sportive tricks,
> Nor made to court an amorous looking-glass;
> . . .
> Cheated of feature by dissembling nature,
> Deform'd, unfinish'd, sent before my time
> Into this breathing world, scarce half made up,
> And that so lamely and unfashionable
> That dogs bark at me as I halt by them;
> Why, I, in this weak piping time of peace,
> Have no delight to pass away the time,
> Unless to spy my shadow in the sun
> And descant on mine own deformity:
> And therefore, since I cannot prove a lover,
> To entertain these fair well-spoken days,
> I am determined to prove a villain
> And hate the idle pleasures of these days.
> Plots have I laid, inductions dangerous,
> By drunken prophecies, libels and dreams,
> To set my brother Clarence and the king
> In deadly hate the one against the other . . .

With a misshapen body (he is later called a "lump of deformity," "a bunch-backed toad"), unsuited to play the lover, and finding no delight in peace, Richard will find his delight in destruction of the peace. Secretly, Richard admits his evil to himself; vigorously, defiantly revels in it; and by dissembling (as he believes nature did with him when she made him), he is determined to be a villain.

Dramatic Monologue The dramatic monologue **is a poem in which one person, in a particular situation, sometimes addressing himself to another person, reveals his private thoughts and emotions.** In Robert Browning's "Caliban upon Setebos" (that is, Caliban's thoughts about his God, Setebos) Caliban, half-man, half-monster, attempts to understand the way God acts by comparing God's actions to the way he, Caliban, would act in a similar position. Believing that Setebos knows his thoughts only when He can see him, Caliban "dances on dark nights" and "gets under holes to laugh,/And never speaks his mind save" as he does now, when hidden in the "cool slush" of a sea-side cave. And yet even now as Caliban speaks, he senses from time to time the presence of Setebos, whom he suspects of listening in on him. Looking out from the privacy of his cave, Caliban observes a line of crabs marching to the sea and he secretly reasons: "Does not God act the way I would with yonder crabs?"

> 'Let twenty pass, and stone the twenty-first,
> Loving not, hating not, just choosing so.
> 'Say, the first straggler that boasts purple spots
> Shall join the file, one pincer twisted off;
> 'Say, this bruised fellow shall receive a worm,
> And two worms he whose nippers end in red;
> As it likes me each time, I do: so He.

What Caliban says is not what his author "means." The author intends that we perceive what Caliban's speech tells us about Caliban. Caliban understands his God to be neither cruel nor kind, but willful and impetuous. By allowing him to think out loud, Browning dramatically shows that Caliban's crude theological musings reveal not God but the low state of the monster's own being. Caliban, throughout the poem, is fearful, envious, dull-witted, spiteful, and amoral. By way of the monologue, insights are given—not only into the monster's theology, into his "natural" religion, but into his mental processes, his feelings and thoughts, his psychological make-up. Your task, then, in reading a monologue is to see through what is said, to the *character* of the person who says it.

In dialogue, soliloquy, dramatic monologue—whenever a character speaks—consciously or unconsciously he reveals himself.

Character's Actions

Character influences action and action reflects character. What a person does mirrors what he is. Because the inner nature of a person affects his external actions, observable actions are clues to unseen emotions.

Flannery O'Connor's short story "Revelation" is about Mrs. Turpin, an opinionated woman who is brought to a painful realization of the low level of her spiritual status—mainly through the actions of another character in the story (the one who initiates Mrs. Turpin's "revelation"), a "fat girl of eighteen or nineteen." As the story opens, Mrs. Turpin enters a doctor's waiting room. Her conversation with the other people in the room reveals her to be prejudiced, self-righteous, hypocritical, narrow, and altogether unconscious of what she is. One of the people in the room is the fat girl, "scowling into a thick blue book . . . her face blue with acne." As Mrs. Turpin talks and reveals her character, the girl acts and reveals hers. At various points during Mrs. Turpin's conversation the fat girl

> looked directly at Mrs. Turpin and smirked . . . returned her eyes to her book . . .turned her lower lip downwards and inside out, revealing the pale pink

inside of her mouth . . . gripped the book in her lap with white fingers . . . turned her lips inside out again . . . made a loud ugly noise through her teeth. . . .

Then Mrs. Turpin turns, once again, to the subject of her good disposition:

"If it's one thing I am . . . it's grateful. When I think who all I could have been besides myself and what all I got, a little of everything, and a good disposition besides, I just feel like shouting, "Thank you, Jesus, for making everything the way it is!" . . .
The book struck her directly over her left eye. It struck almost at the same instant that she realized the girl was about to hurl it. Before she could utter a sound, the raw face came crashing across the table toward her, howling. The girl's fingers sank like clamps into the soft flesh of her neck.

With a minimum of comment the author presents the main feature of the girl's character—not through an explanation of it, or through another character's comments about it, or through anything the girl herself says (except her "howling"), but through the girl's actions. Had the girl's actions not been shown, we would not have been so aware of the depth of the emotion hidden in her.

To illustrate character an author may use deceptively simple actions. An action may be little more than a gesture and yet still convey a state of mind, the hidden world of character. "What is character but the determination of incident?" Henry James wrote. "What is incident but the illustration of character? . . . It is an incident for a woman to stand up with her hand resting on a table and look out at you in a certain way. . . . At the same time it is an expression of character." A girl trying to choke someone, a woman with her "hand resting on a table"—both actions demonstrate character. Both show emotion in action.

When reading for character, you may begin by asking yourself such questions as the following: What does the author say about the character? What do the other characters say about him? In what ways does the character's talk reveal him? How do his actions expose his inner nature? By asking such questions you may find a starting point for a detailed study of character.

Reading Techniques

When you are studying the relationships of **many different characters** within a work, you may find marking the names of the characters and underlining their individual characteristics a good beginning. When you are making a study of **one character** in a work, listing the character's various personality traits can provide a good summary for analysis. When you are studying **one dominant characteristic of one character** in a work, diagramming the different manifestations of that characteristic helps clarify it.

Marking Different Characters

When studying many different characters within a work, simply putting a box or circle around the names of characters when they appear and underlining their significant traits will help clarify the dramatis personae of the work and will allow you, when you return to them for special study, to find them at a glance.

In some novels a character and the author's description of him may appear on one page and then the character will not reappear until some pages later. And yet to understand the relationship of characters within the novel, the reader must remember the character and his essential characteristics.

In Jane Austen's *Pride and Prejudice* the main characters are the five Bennet girls, their suitors, and their suitors' relatives. Confusion about characters and their characteristics can be alleviated by marking. Following is an example of how passages describing the two principal characters, Fitzwilliam Darcy and Elizabeth Bennet, might be marked.

[Mr. Darcy] soon drew the attention of the room by his _fine_, _tall person_, _handsome features_, _noble_ mien; and the report which was in general circulation within five minutes after his entrance, of his having _ten thousand a year_ . . . till _his manners gave a disgust_ which turned the tide of his popularity, for he was discovered to be _proud_. . . .

[Elizabeth]'s face . . . was rendered uncommonly _intelligent_ by the _beautiful expression_ of her _dark eyes_. . . . [Darcy] was forced to acknowledge her _figure_ to be _light and pleasing_; and in spite of his asserting that her _manners_ were not those of the fashionable world, he was caught by their _easy playfulness_.

Listing Characteristics

If you are doing a detailed study of one character, you may find it helpful to list his outstanding characteristics. The qualities of Clarence E. Mulford's Hopalong Cassidy, for example, are many and varied. By simply describing them and quoting a short passage as evidence, you provide a picture of the man in the round.

Knowledgeable: "Nobody on Gawd's gray earth knows how much that feller knows!"

Nonchalant and astute: . . . a shot roared out, almost deafening him. . . . Hopalong removed his sombrero and looked at the hole near the edge of the brim . . . inserting the tip of his little finger into it. . . . "Yeah, it was close," he said slowly, grinning grimly. "At first I reckoned mebby it might be an old one; but that hole in the wall says it ain't."

Wary: Hopalong's fingers were calloused, but the backs of his fingers were not; and he now bunched his cards in his left hand, face to the palm, and let the backs of the fingers of his right hand brush gently down the involved patterns, searching for pin pricks.

Enjoys a high degree of manual dexterity: ... but other men had discovered, when too late, that Hopalong's left hand was the better of the two. The double roar seemed to bend the walls, and sent the lamp flames leaping, to flicker almost to extinction. ... The smoke thinned to show Hawes sliding from his chair. ...

Diagramming a Dominant Characteristic

With almost any work of literature you can gain new insights by seeing how the central character manifests himself in relation to (1) other characters, (2) the major events of the work, (3) his own inner conflicts, (4) the world order—that is, the author's assumptions about the laws governing the universe as they are shown to exist within the context of the work.

Figure 1 shows one possible way of using this method to study Achilleus, the main character in Homer's epic poem *The Iliad*. The opening stanza of *The Iliad* states the subject: "Sing, goddess, the anger of Peleus' son Achilleus and its devastation." At the center of *The Iliad* is the anger of Achilleus. By putting this emotion at the center of other elements in the story, the reader may gain a clearer picture of it.

Figure 1   Diagramming a Dominant Characteristic

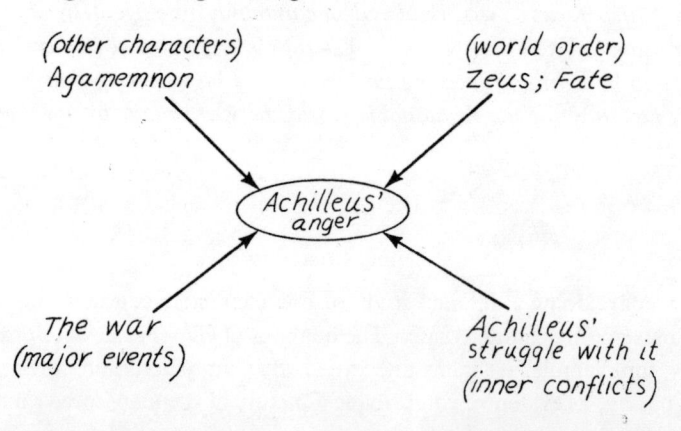

```
(other characters)              (world order)
Agamemnon                       Zeus; Fate
         \                      /
          \                    /
           → ( Achilleus' ) ←
              anger
          /                    \
         /                      \
The war                         Achilleus'
(major events)                  struggle with it
                                (inner conflicts)
```

Achilleus' Anger and Agamemnon   Near the conclusion of the ten-year seige of Troy by the Greeks, a quarrel occurs between the two Greek chiefs, Agamemnon and Achilleus. Agamemnon believes he has the authority to take Achilleus' captive mistress, Briseis, for his own; Achilleus argues that the spoils have been distributed and should not be called back. Agamemnon replies, "I shall take the fair-cheeked Briseis . . . I myself going to your shelter, that you may learn well how much greater I am than you. . . ." Achilleus' anger arises:

> And the anger came on Peleus' son, and within
> his shaggy breast the heart was divided two ways, pondering
> whether to draw from beside his thigh the sharp sword, driving
> away all those who stood between and kill the son of Atreus,
> or else to check the spleen within and keep down his anger.

Achilleus' Anger and the War   The hate generated in Achilleus by his quarrel with Agamemnon expands to include his emotional relation to the war itself. He will fight no more and prays that without him the Greeks will be defeated. His anger now takes the form of self-pity and sorrow and drives Achilleus away from the war he loves: "Achilleus weeping went and sat in sorrow apart from his companions beside the beach of the grey sea looking out on the infinite water."

Without Achilleus the Greeks fall before the Trojan power, led by "man-slaughtering Hektor." Patroclus, Achilleus' closest friend, goes to fight in Achilleus' place and is killed by Hektor. Now Achilleus' anger surmounts his hate for Agamemnon and his hate for the Greek cause and turns on Hektor and the Trojans. And he goes to battle: "shining in all his armour like the sun when it crosses above us." Achilleus slays Hektor. But so great is his rage that it is not appeased with his enemy's death:

> Then, when he had yoked running horses under the chariot
> he would fasten Hektor behind the chariot, so as to drag him,
> and draw him three times around the tomb of Menoitios' fallen
> son [Patroclus], then rest again in his shelter, and throw down the dead man
> and leave him to lie sprawled on his face in the dust.

In this desecration of Hektor's body, Achilleus "does dishonour to the dumb earth in his fury." His anger has carried him beyond wounded pride, self-pity, sorrow, and revenge.

Achilleus' Struggles with His Anger   Priam, Hektor's aged father, comes to Achilleus' shelter to ransom his son's body. So great is Priam's grief that Achilleus, remembering his own father, weeps for both his own and Hektor's father, who now kneels before him. But when Priam counsels Achilleus to give him Hektor's body, Achilleus' anger again rises:

> Then looking darkly at him spoke swift-footed Achilleus:
> "No longer stir me up, old sir. I myself am minded
> to give Hektor back to you. . . .
>   Therefore
> you must not further make my spirit move in my sorrows,
> for fear, old sir, I might not let you alone in my shelter."

Even at this moment of pity for Priam, anger still works in Achilleus. But now, with his sense of their common grief, Achilleus is able to exercise a measure of control over the flaw in his character.

Achilleus' Anger and The World Order (Zeus and Fate)   The primary source, perhaps, of Achilleus' anger is his inability to accept his fate. Before he came to Troy, Achilleus was given a choice: Either he could stay in Greece and, without glory, live quietly to a comfortable old age; or he could sail to Troy and win undying fame in a short life. His mother tells him, "it has befallen that your life must be brief and bitter beyond all men's." It is this destiny that Achilleus cannot accept—unless others pay him the great honor he feels he deserves.

But now, alone in his shelter with Priam, Achilleus reveals a large emotional acceptance of his own life.

> There are two urns that stand on the door-sill of Zeus. They are unlike
> for the gifts they bestow: an urn of evils, an urn of blessings.
> If Zeus who delights in thunder mingles these and bestows them
> on man, he shifts, and moves now in evil, again in good fortune.
> But when Zeus bestows from the urn of sorrows, he makes a failure
> of man, and the evil hunger drives him over the shining
> earth, and he wanders respected neither of gods nor mortals.

Achilleus has come to understand his own life, not in relation to Agamemnon or the war or a personal weakness, but within the compass of the unalterable condition of man's life on earth. Achilleus attains an equilibrium within himself which his anger and pride have prevented until now.

By studying Achilleus' anger, the subject of *The Iliad,* in its relation to major characters (Agamemnon, Hektor, Priam . . .), to events (the war, Patroclus' death), to Achilleus' own struggles with it, and to the laws governing the universe, the reader may approach an understanding of the thought and emotion of the entire epic.

You can analyze a major character in almost any work of literature by putting that character at the center of the various elements that make up his world. Such a study may lead you to a clearer picture of the total work.

Writing Suggestions

Beginning a paper is often a matter of finding material to work with. Before you start to write, you may need to go through the work you have been reading to look for clues that will help you decide on a topic.

Perhaps you have found a character who is of particular interest to you. By asking yourself some basic questions, you may find that the character's external appearance or his internal psychological make-up provide a basis for character analysis.

> *What does the character look like?—red beefsteak face? a thin blue vein running across her forehead? . . .*
> *How does he dress (does the shell reveal the tortoise)?—a coat of fastidious black and white spats? gray stockings, a red skirt, and a bibbed apron? . . .*
> *What words are used to describe him?—breaker-of-horses? slow-witted? . .*
> *What does he say?—"I'll eat my head if I'm wrong"? "You see me falling back but only for a spring forward"? . . .*
> *What general type does the character fall into?—demoniac? braggart-bully? . . .*
> *What elements within him are in conflict?—anger and pity? love and hate? . . .*
> *What are his opinions?—"Women are no damn good"? "A strand of a woman's hair is worth all the philosophers who ever lived"? . . .*

What goes on in his hidden world?—"*Little do these puppets know how I control them*"? "*He thinks I think him honest*"? . . .
How is his mind described?—*as a vast desert lake a few inches deep at its deepest point? as a room with three chairs in it, in which an idea has entered and seated itself on all three chairs at once?* . . .

The central idea for your paper may grow out of the detailed thinking that the above questions call for. And your central idea will need to be supported by specific details similar to those given above. When writing about a flat character, you will need to indicate in what way he is static and how the idea he represents functions within the work.

A round character can be approached from different angles. You can explain the relationship between the character and the action of the story, or you can describe the various aspects of the character's personality—his desires, emotions, opinions, secret thoughts—that make him the many-sided, contradictory representation of a human being he is.

By studying the ways an author reveals character, you may discover your topic: (1) What does the author say about the character? (2) What do other characters say about him? (3) What does the character himself say? (4) What does he do?

Because you cannot always explicitly believe what an author says or what characters do or say, you may need to do some detective work to uncover the underlying reason for their talking or acting in a certain way. If you are able to see through the action to the thought and emotion behind it, then what a person does will mirror what he is, even if he attempts to cover up his real motives.

By putting the character at the center of the created world that surrounds him, you may gain a wealth of material for a theme topic: How does the character manifest himself in relation to (1) other characters, (2) major events, (3) his own inner states, (4) the world in which he lives?

Plot

2

To read for plot is to read for more than the action of a literary work; to write about plot is to write about more than what happens. **PLOT** is not merely a series of occurrences but is **an arranged sequence of interrelated events that lead somewhere.** Because it is part of an organic whole, because it is a synthesis of action, character, and thought, plot cannot be detached and isolated from other aspects of a work of literature. Reading for plot is one way of beginning to understand the whole work.

The following discussion of the anonymous poem "Frankie and Johnny" describes the interrelationship of incidents within a plot. The first stanza of the poem states the subject: Frankie and Johnny's love.

> Frankie and Johnny were lovers, O, how that couple could love,
> Swore to be true to each other, true as the stars above.
> He was her man, but he done her wrong.

The next three stanzas give specific details that reveal the nature of this love.

> Frankie she was his woman, everybody knows.
> She spent one hundred dollars for a suit of Johnny's clothes.
> He was her man, but he done her wrong.
>
> Frankie and Johnny went walking, Johnny in his bran' new suit
> "O good Lawd," says Frankie, "but don't my Johnny look cute?"
> He was her man, but he done her wrong.
>
> Frankie went down to Memphis; she went on the evening train.
> She paid one hundred dollars for Johnny a watch and chain.
> He was her man, but he done her wrong.

Frankie's actions (buying the suit, the watch, and exclaiming "don't my Johnny look cute?") show the strength of Frankie's active love and tell us, perhaps something about Johnny's desires and interests (his clothing and his looks). These first four stanzas mark the **EXPOSITION** or **INTRODUCTION**. This part of the plot **gives the necessary information in preparation for the events that are to follow.**

The next two stanzas, by way of direct action and dialogue, provoke a change in the situation presented in the exposition.

> Frankie went down to the corner, to buy a glass of beer;
> She says to the bartender, "Has my loving man been here?
> He is my man; he wouldn't do me wrong."
>
> "Ain't going to tell you no story, ain't going to tell you no lie,
> I seen your man 'bout an hour ago with a girl named Alice Fry.
> If he's your man, he's doing you wrong."

In this part of the narrative a **COMPLICATION** occurs. **A tension, a problem suddenly exists.** This love that was as "true as the stars above" is now as untrue as the humans below. The stable situation presented in the exposition is now unstable. Things cannot now remain the way they are. The reader wonders how Frankie will react and what the outcome will be.

The next scene suggests the outcome of the tension that has arisen in the complication and discloses a new aspect of Frankie's character.

> Frankie went back to the hotel, she didn't go there for fun,
> Under her long red kimono she toted a forty-four gun.
> He was her man, he was doing her wrong.

In the following scenes the problem presented in the complication is rapidly and decisively resolved.

> Frankie went down to the hotel, looked in the window so high,
> There was her lovin' Johnny a-lovin' up Alice Fry;
> He was her man, he was doing her wrong.
>
> Frankie threw back her kimono; took out the old forty-four;
> Roota-toot-toot, three times she shot, right through that hotel door.
> She shot her man, 'cause he done her wrong.
>
> Johnny grabbed off his Stetson. "O good Lawd, Frankie, don't
>   shoot."
> But Frankie put her finger on the trigger, and the gun went
>   roota-toot-toot.
> He was her man, but she shot him down.
>
> "Roll me over easy, roll me over slow,
> Roll me over easy, boys, 'cause my wounds is hurting me so,
> I was her man, but I done her wrong."

When Frankie finds Johnny with Alice, Frankie acts to resolve this undesirable and unstable situation. And when Frankie shoots "roota-toot-toot," the **CRISIS** occurs; that is, **the decisive incident** is given **which marks the high point of the action** begun in the complication. The **CLIMAX** may occur here also if this moment is **the high point of the reader's emotional response to the narrative.** (CRISIS refers to an incident in the story, CLIMAX to the reader's response.)

Immediately following the crisis, there is, perhaps, a part of the plot called the **RECOGNITION—that moment when a character sees the true condition of his existence.** When Johnny says, "I was her man, but I done her wrong," he may be realizing for the first time what the refrain, the last line of each stanza, has been saying all along. He may now be aware of something which he was never completely aware of before.

In the final stanza the problem presented in the complication finds its solution.

"Oh, bring on your rubber-tired hearses, bring on your rubber-tired hacks,
They're takin' Johnny to the buryin' groun' but they'll never bring him back.
He was my man, but he done me wrong."

This is **the outcome of the conflict—**the **CATASTROPHE** or **DENOUEMENT**. Everything is settled; **a new stability in the situation is reached.** The story of Frankie and Johnny's love is ended.

Plot, then, is a synthesis of such story elements as action, character, and theme. When Johnny saw Frankie with the gun, he "grabbed off his Stetson." This action tells us something about Johnny's character. The interaction of the events of the whole narrative, moreover, say something about such abstract subjects as justice, love, retribution, vanity, human nature, and human relationships.

In all plots, it should be noted, there is **CONFLICT, a struggle between two opposing forces** (man against man, man against society, man against the forces of nature, man against the laws of the universe, man against opposing forces within himself). "Frankie and Johnny" is an example of the first of these conflicts—woman against her man.

In all plots there is an underlying logic—a cause, an effect, a psychological reason for the happenings. Frankie shoots Johnny *because* they are sworn to love each other and he is found violating this love. *Because* Johnny is the kind of man he is, he violates their love. And *because* Frankie is the kind of woman she is, she shoots him. Action reveals character; character determines action. One thing brings on another.

All plots have a **BEGINNING,** a **MIDDLE,** and an **END.** If we had only the beginning, Frankie and Johnny sworn true to each other, there would be no plot. If we had only the middle, Johnny "a-lovin' up Alice," or only the end, Johnny in his hearse, there would be no plot.

Any one plot can, of course, be looked at in a number of different ways. Another way of viewing the plot of "Frankie and Johnny" is to see how it consists of a **RISING** action and a **FALLING** action. Looked at in this manner, a plot can be divided into six parts (see Figure 2).

Whatever method you use to analyze plot, the essential questions to ask yourself are **How** are the events related? and **Why** do they happen? The terms **exposition, exciting force, complication, rising action, crisis, falling action, climax, recognition, denouement** may prove helpful to you if you use them not with the intention of simply naming parts (experts may not agree on the specific application of these terms to one particular work) but for the purpose of becoming more aware of how

Figure 2 Plot

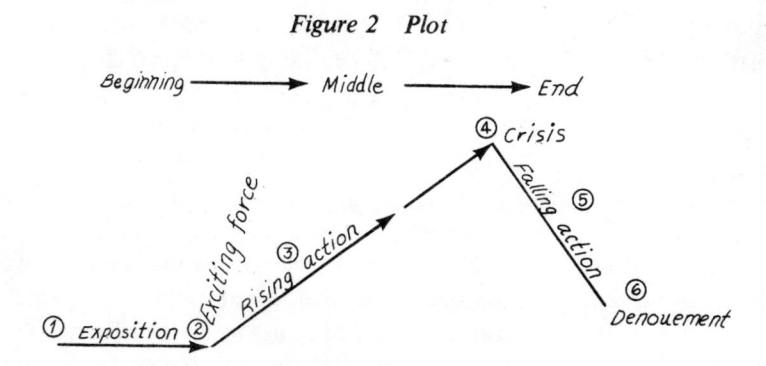

```
Beginning ——————→ Middle ——————→ End
                                    ④ Crisis
                            ③ action
                        Rising
                                      ⑤ Falling action
              ② Exciting force
                                            ⑥
   ① Exposition                          Denouement
```

1. **Exposition** *or* **Introduction** *Leading characters are introduced, and dominant emotional relationships between them given: Frankie and Johnny are lovers. Frankie buys Johnny suit, watch, and chain.*
2. **Exciting Force** *Incident that upsets stable situation of* exposition, *begins the* complication, *and sets in conflict two opposing forces: Frankie learns that Johnny is with Alice; Frankie's true love is set in conflict with Johnny's fickle love.*
3. **Rising action** *Begins with the* exciting force. *Suspense, expectation of possible resolution of tension between opposing forces. Conflict develops: Frankie goes to hotel, forty-four under red kimono; Frankie looks in window, sees Johnny and Alice.*
4. **Crisis** *Incident that marks turning point, reversal in action.* Rising Action *becomes* Falling Action. *Conflict of opposing forces must now be resolved: Frankie shoots Johnny (Johnny now receives not the gifts of the* exposition *but the bullets of the* crisis*).*
5. **Falling Action** *Begins with the* crisis. *Resolution of tension between opposing forces is given: Johnny grabs off Stetson, asks to be rolled over easy, says, "I done her wrong."*
6. **Denouement** *Logical outcome of the action. A stability different from the stability of the* exposition *is the result of the conflict between opposing forces: Final view of Johnny being rolled away in hearse to the stability of the "buryin' groun'."*

you yourself understand the interrelation and interaction of the parts of a narrative. Though most of these terms were originally used to describe the component elements of classical drama, they are also applicable to most narrative and epic poetry and to most short stories, novels, and plays. If you do not force their application, these terms will lead you beyond a mere summary of the action of a work.

Not all plots, of course, are as simple or obvious as the "Frankie and Johnny" plot. Of the many different kinds of plots you will read, two may prove especially difficult to analyze: the multiple plot (a work may contain not one but many plots) and the modern anti-plot (a story may appear to have no plot at all).

The Multiple Plot

In *A Midsummer Night's Dream* Shakespeare treats the subject of love from different standpoints by interweaving the actions of four different sets of lovers:

the kingly, mature love of Theseus, Duke of Athens, and Hippolyta, Queen of the Amazons; the confused, emotional love of two pairs of Athenian youths Lysander and Hermia, Demetruis and Helena; the jealous, quarrelsome love of Oberon, King of the Fairies, and Titania, his Queen; the tragic-romantic love (portrayed by a group of thick-witted actors) of a pair of ancient lovers, Pyramus and Thisbe. Each set of lovers has its own plot, which comments on and emphasizes the others. The author begins one plot (the Theseus-Hippolyta love story), introduces another (the Demetrius-Helena-Lysander-Hermia love triangles), and then another (the Oberon-Titania love conflict), reintroduces the second, runs them all along parallel to each other, intersects them at various points, and brings to climax a fourth (the dramatic Thisbe and Pyramus love feast). In the conclusion to the play, he ties all four plots together to dramatize a unified but complex experience of love.

When analyzing a multiple plot, you will need to read carefully—first, to follow each individual plot along its way and, second, to see in what ways each plot is an antithesis, a synthesis, or a complement of each of the other plots.

The Modern Anti-Plot

Writers in the tradition of Chekhov, Katherine Mansfield, and James Joyce stress the influence of environment and the inner psychological responses of their characters while deemphasizing dramatic action. Because theirs is the "technique of understatement," because they have "detheatricalized" their stories, the beginnings and ends to their plots are not clearly defined. There are no gouging of eyes with golden brooches, no armies marching, no dead bodies left on stage—only a little old maid attending a Halloween party and returning home. Chekhov expressed the idea for the anti-plot this way: "Why write about a man getting into a submarine and going to the North Pole to reconcile himself to the world, while his beloved at that moment throws herself with a hysterical shriek from the belfry? . . . One must write about simple things: how Peter Semionovich married Maria Ivanovna. That is all."

To give an impression of the day-by-day frustrations and to render the poverty of the day-by-day existence of ordinary people, the modern author may select actions as insignificant as the main character's in James Joyce's *Ulysses:* "He laid the dry snot picked from his nostril on a ledge, carefully." This action and many others like it reveal character and develop the idea of the novel. In Katherine Mansfield's "The Fly" the central character becomes identified with a struggling ink-soaked fly on his desk and drops blots of ink from his pen onto the fly until the "black legs . . . stuck to the body." This action marks the climax of the story and exposes the state of the protagonist's being and the level of his consciousness.

Because of the absence of large dramatic action, plot in the modern story may easily be overlooked. Complication and climax, however, are almost always present. To be aware of them you may need to pay special attention to some apparently insignificant actions. (A method for analyzing the anti-plot follows under Reading Techniques.)

Reading Techniques

Though many plots may be analyzed according to the method used for the "Frankie and Johnny" plot given at the beginning of this chapter, many plots do not lend themselves to such formal analyses. You may find the following less complex method of clarifying action more practical for your purposes.

When you read for plot, two of the first things to look for are (1) the point of change or reversal in the main character's fortunes or outlook on life, (2) the high point of your own emotional response to the narrative. These two points may coincide, but in some stories they may not. In plots in which there is no major change (as in the modern anti-plot), it is still necessary to know at which point your highest emotional response occurs.

One way to discover these important points in a story is to outline, diagram, or mark outstanding events. By using these techniques to simplify the action, you may arrive at new insights into *why* such and such happens *when* it does. In the two examples that follow, methods are suggested to help clarify two kinds of plots. In the first example the change in the character's outlook on life is a gradual one. In the second example nothing changes for the character, and the reader's response to the story depends on his realization of this fact.

Outlining and Diagramming the Plot of Gradual Change

Authors often outline the sequence of events before beginning the actual writing of individual scenes. Dickens, for example, used an outline ("Number Plans," he called them) to guide him through the writing of *David Copperfield*. A reader can benefit by beginning his study of a work of literature in much the same way that Dickens and many other authors began work on their stories.

In Nathaniel Hawthorne's short story "Young Goodman Brown" the main character makes a journey through the woods one night outside his native village of Salem. Goodman's journey is punctuated by a series of meetings with townspeople, each of whom he has "reverenced from youth" and each of whom he later finds gathered in the numerous congregation which is joined in a hymn, united in the brotherhood of evil that seems to exist in all mankind. "And now my children, look upon each other," the leader of the congregation says as four pine trees blaze with unholy fire, and Goodman becomes "more conscious of the secret guilt of others, both in deed and thought. ..."

Here is one possible skeletal outline of the story.

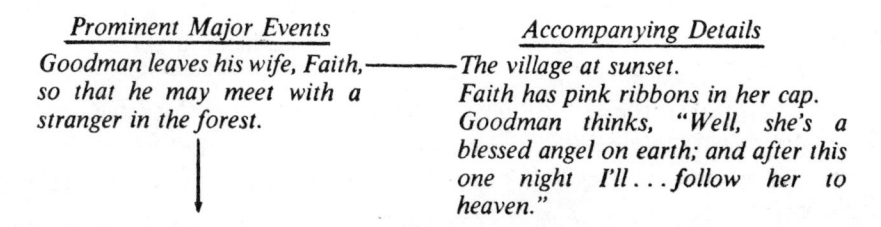

Prominent Major Events	*Accompanying Details*
Goodman leaves his wife, Faith, so that he may meet with a stranger in the forest.	The village at sunset. Faith has pink ribbons in her cap. Goodman thinks, "Well, she's a blessed angel on earth; and after this one night I'll... follow her to heaven."

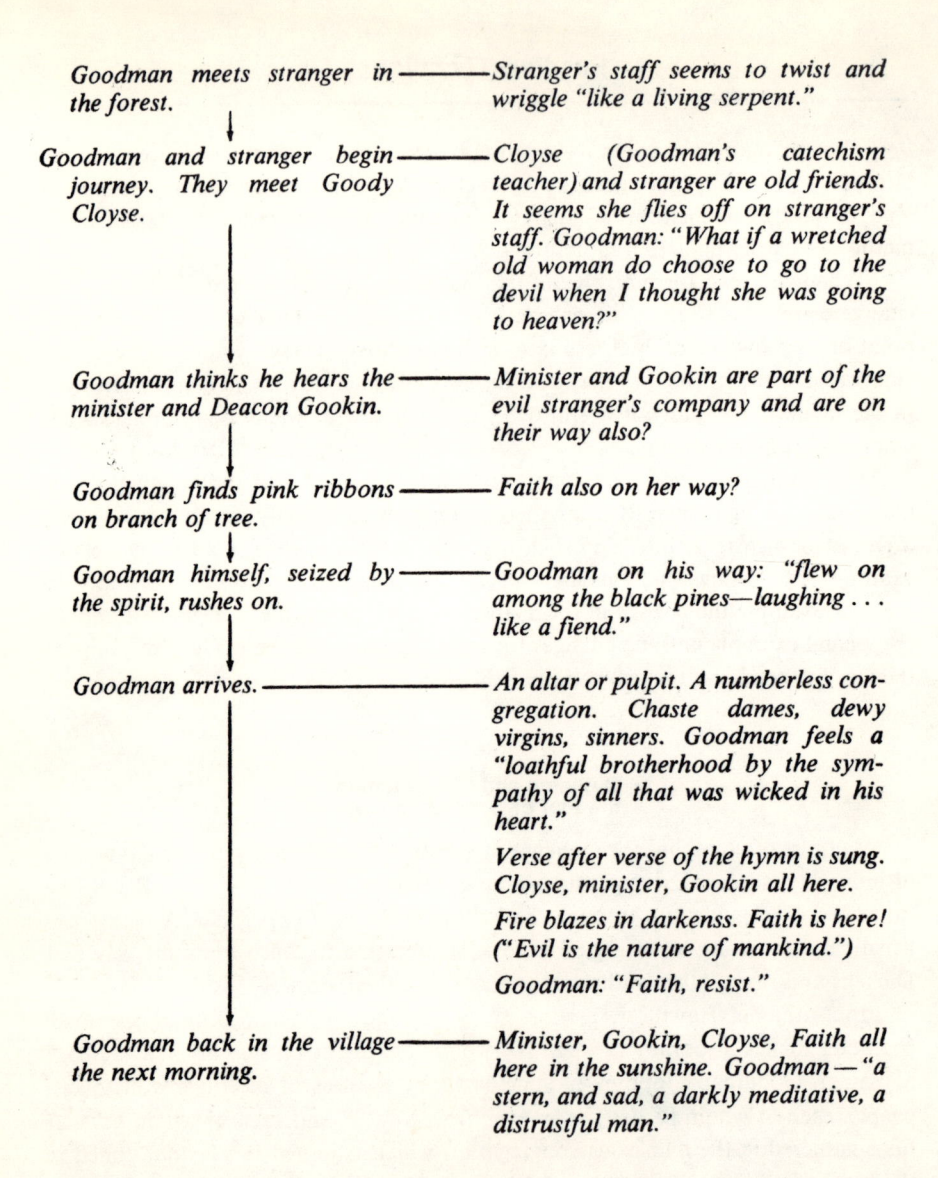

Goodman meets stranger in the forest.	—*Stranger's staff seems to twist and wriggle "like a living serpent."*
Goodman and stranger begin journey. They meet Goody Cloyse.	—*Cloyse (Goodman's catechism teacher) and stranger are old friends. It seems she flies off on stranger's staff. Goodman: "What if a wretched old woman do choose to go to the devil when I thought she was going to heaven?"*
Goodman thinks he hears the minister and Deacon Gookin.	—*Minister and Gookin are part of the evil stranger's company and are on their way also?*
Goodman finds pink ribbons on branch of tree.	—*Faith also on her way?*
Goodman himself, seized by the spirit, rushes on.	—*Goodman on his way: "flew on among the black pines—laughing . . . like a fiend."*
Goodman arrives.	—*An altar or pulpit. A numberless congregation. Chaste dames, dewy virgins, sinners. Goodman feels a "loathful brotherhood by the sympathy of all that was wicked in his heart."*
	Verse after verse of the hymn is sung. Cloyse, minister, Gookin all here.
	Fire blazes in darkenss. Faith is here! ("Evil is the nature of mankind.")
	Goodman: "Faith, resist."
Goodman back in the village the next morning.	—*Minister, Gookin, Cloyse, Faith all here in the sunshine. Goodman—"a stern, and sad, a darkly meditative, a distrustful man."*

This outline reveals that Hawthorne's story is made up of a series of happenings which show a number of changes and perhaps one final complete change in the emotions of the main character. Goodman feels one way at the beginning of the story, another at the end. The cause for the change in Goodman is brought about by the journey he has taken through the woods that night.

The symmetry of Hawthorne's tale emphasizes the change in Goodman. Action begins in the village and ends in the village. Goodman leaves Faith at sunset thinking his wife is a "blessed angel" and returns at sunrise a "darkly meditative man." Figure 3 shows how the story could be diagrammed.

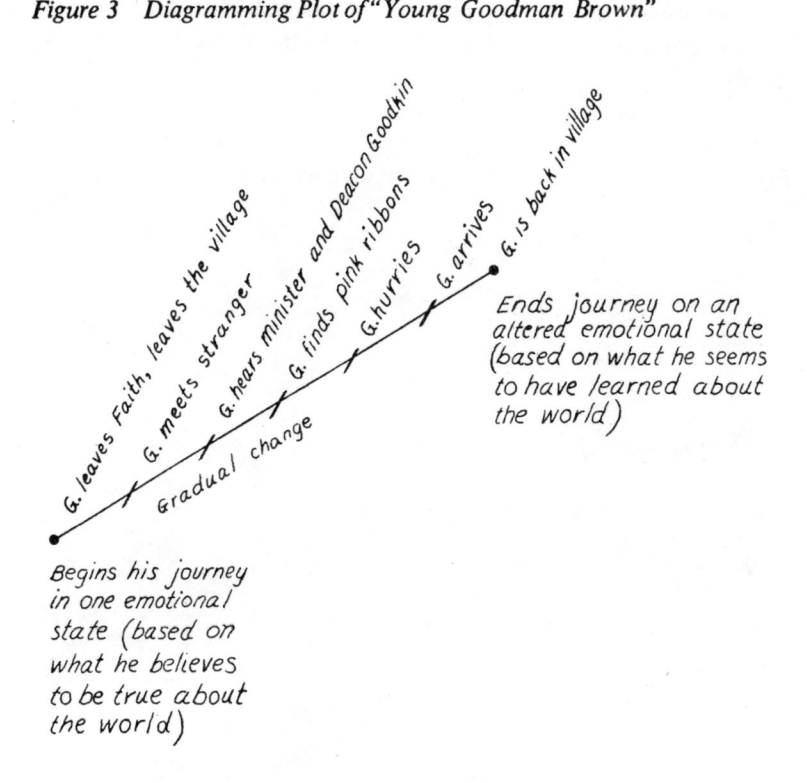

Figure 3   Diagramming Plot of "Young Goodman Brown"

G. leaves Faith, leaves the village
G. meets stranger
G. hears minister and Deacon Goodkin
G. finds pink ribbons
G. hurries
G. arrives
G. is back in village
Gradual change

Ends journey on an altered emotional state (based on what he seems to have learned about the world)

Begins his journey in one emotional state (based on what he believes to be true about the world)

Diagramming the Anti-Plot

The anti-plot is sometimes called the plot of no change. A straight horizontal line rather than a gradually ascending line would be a more accurate indication of this kind of story.

The action of Anton Chekhov's "In the Cart" begins with Marya Vasilyevna in a cart. She is being driven out of town by old Semyon. The sun is splendid, the sky "marvelous, immeasurably deep." But Marya feels no joy. She has been teaching school for thirteen years and has made this trip many times to the neighboring town to collect her salary.

On the road Marya's cart is overtaken by another cart. It is the rich landowner Hanov. He is a bachelor with "a worn face and a lifeless expression ... a weak creature, already blighted." For Marya "life is passing drearily, without warmth. ..." It occurs to her that "if she were his wife ... she would devote her whole life to his rescue."

Marya and old Semyon drive on to Gorodishche. They drink tea in a sweaty, noisy, foul-smelling teahouse. They make the journey back to their village of Vyazovye. Just outside the village the cart stops at a railroad crossing. Marya gets out of the cart. A train is passing. She catches a glimpse of a lady on the train and she is reminded of her mother and imagines the life she, Marya, lived thirteen years before. "A feeling of joy overwhelmed her." Hanov drives up, and "seeing him she imagined such happiness as had never been. ..."

"Vasilyevna, get in!" Semyon calls. Marya gets back in the cart and returns to the life that has "aged and coarsened her, making her homely, angular, and clumsy...."

That is all there is to the story. Marya does not marry Hanov. There is no change in her life, no reversal of fortune—only the commonplace events of a dull existence. Figure 4 shows how the story might be diagrammed.

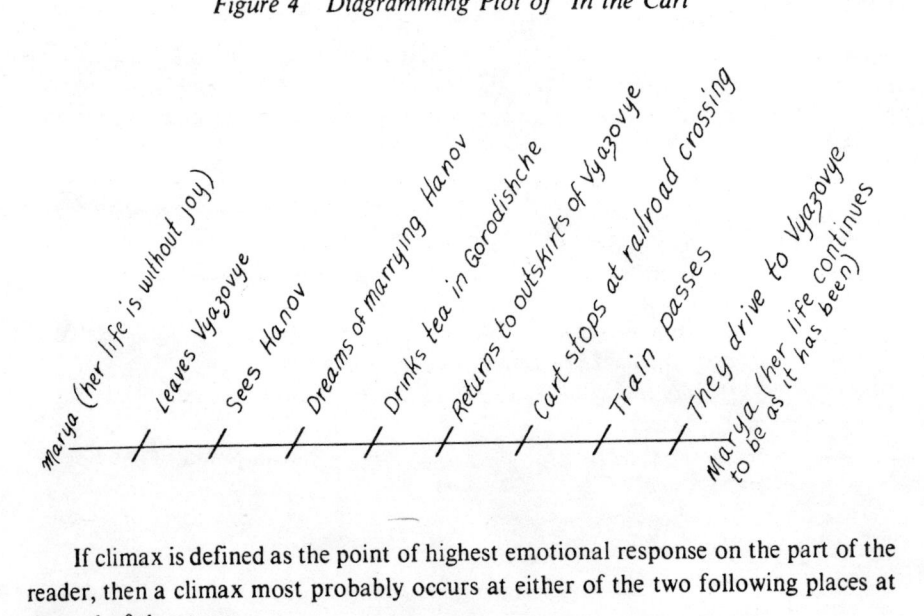

Figure 4   Diagramming Plot of "In the Cart"

Marya (her life is without joy) / Leaves Vyazovye / Sees Hanov / Dreams of marrying Hanov / Drinks tea in Gorodishche / Returns to outskirts of Vyazovye / Cart stops at railroad crossing / Train passes / They drive to Vyazovye / Marya (her life continues to be as it has been)

If climax is defined as the point of highest emotional response on the part of the reader, then a climax most probably occurs at either of the two following places at the end of the story:

[As the train passes and Marya imagines her former life:]
A feeling of joy and happiness suddenly overwhelmed her, she pressed her hand to her temples in ecstasy, and called softly, imploringly: "Mama!"

[or]

[After the train passes, Marya returns to her present life:]
And suddenly it all vanished. The barrier was slowly rising. Marya Vasilyevna, shivering and numb with cold, got into the cart.... "And this is Vyazovye. Here we are."

The action in both these passages is trivial in comparison to the action of classical drama. And yet the reader may respond with a great deal of emotion to either of these passages, which render the emptiness and pain of Marya's existence and the lack of change in it. This is the way Marya's life was before the story began, and this is the way it will be after it ends.

The conflict in this story (as is often the case in the modern anti-plot) is between the main character and society, and also between two opposing psychological forces within the main character. The cultural world in which Marya finds herself opposes her desires (as nearly unconscious as they are unrealized) for a fuller life. The pain within Marya grows out of her deep emotional longing for happiness and (as we know from the insights given into her consciousness) from the frustration resulting from the complete absence of the attainment of such happiness.

Writing Suggestions

When you write about plot, you will need to do more than restate the action. Not the events themselves but their relationship, their interaction with each other, is a subject for a paper. To discover the dynamics of the plot you are studying, you might ask yourself the following questions, answering them as specifically as possible so that you will have exact details to support all generalizations.

What is the high point of your emotional response to the story?—when the mother strokes the bald path on the father's head? when the main character drops through the floorboards into a pot of boiling oil? . . .
What are the main events?—the king is murdered? the maid buys some shoes? . . .
What does the main character want?—to free the city from the plague? to prove to himself that he has courage? . . .
What does he do to get it?—searches for the unclean thing? kills the buffalo? . . .
What does he do when he gets it?—blinds himself? finds the confidence he was looking for? . . .
What befalls him after he gets what he wanted?—he is banished? his wife shoots him? . . .
What events have led up to an incident and caused it?—a fly falls into an inkwell? the boy's father performs an egg trick? . . .
What events follow as a result of it?—the kingdom is restored? a boy is left a social misfit? . . .
What does the action mean?—man is living in hell? man is living in paradise but doesn't know it? . . .

Because conflict is essential to plot, a paper analyzing the basic conflict in a work may lead to an exposition of the plot. The idea for your paper may arise out of the reason the conflict exists at all, or the reason it concludes the way it does. In most cases you will need to discuss the motivations of the main character.

You may find one point in a story which claims your highest emotional response. Analysis of this high point, the events leading up to it, and those following it provide material for a critical paper.

It will be necessary, you should remember, to limit your analysis to one event and its cause and effects or to a few major incidents and their interrelation.

Setting

3

In its narrowest sense **SETTING is the place and time of the action:** the Greek city of Thebes some time in remote antiquity; hell, purgatory, and paradise in 1300; Spain during the Renaissance; trees overlooking apartment windows at night in twentieth-century America. Such simple statements of setting tell us little about Sophocles' *Oedipus Rex,* Dante's *Divine Comedy,* Cervantes' *Don Quixote,* or James Dickey's "The Fiend."

In a larger sense **SETTING is the background, the social environment, the atmosphere of a literary work; the interrelationship of place and time with action, character, and thought; the contribution of place and time to the achievement of the total work.**

Functions of Setting

Setting may function in a number of different ways. It can, for example, (1) cause action, (2) affect character, (3) reveal character, (4) serve as background for the action, (5) represent a state of mind.

Setting as It Causes Action

The relationship between setting and action is often so obvious that is is overlooked: the mountain, the river, the house are there, and the character climbs it, swims it, lives in it.

In *The Odyssey* the hero, Odysseus, wants to return home to his wife and his kingdom. In one incident from Book Twelve of the epic there lies in the path of Odysseus' ship a mountain of polished stone and a tongue of land. Within the mountain is the den of Skylla, a monster with six long necks and six heads, each with three rows of teeth. From out of the black gullets of her six throats Skylla yaps like a hound dog. Below the tongue of land lurks the whirlpool of Kharybdis, who swallows the sea and discharges it in a horrible whirlpool. Odysseus must sail between them.

> Next we began to sail up the narrow strait lamenting. For on the one hand lay Scylla, and on the other mighty Charybdis in terrible wise sucked down the salt sea water. . . . Towards her, then, we looked fearing destruction; but Scylla meanwhile caught from out my hollow ship six of my company, the hardiest of their hands and the chief in might . . . they cried aloud in their agony, and called me by my name for that last time of all.

Skylla and Kharybdis are there and Odysseus acts: he sails between them and hears the voices of six of his men call down to him "in anguish." The setting—the place after place after place that Odysseus touches on in his wanderings in the tenth year of his homeward voyage from Troy to Ithaca—is a major factor in the movement, the action, and the liveliness of the epic. It can be said that setting is the primary cause of the action in *The Odyssey*.

The "action" of a literary work may be not so much the actions of a single character but the actions of all the characters, a whole culture as it responds to its total environment. The Egyptian civilization, it has been said, was the result of an action made in response to the challenge of the Nile. And in a similar way, an ocean, a desert, a prairie, a tropical forest may be the primary cause for the action in a piece of fiction.

The questions to ask yourself, then, are what in the setting presents a problem or challenges the characters, and how do they respond?

Setting as It Affects Character

Not only may setting cause a character to act, but it may affect or determine character; that is, the mental and emotional qualities of a person may be a consequence of the place and time of his existence. A character may *be* the way he is because of the physical world that surrounds him.

In Lawrence Durrell's *The Alexandria Quartet,* one of the characters says, "We live . . . lives based upon selected fictions. Our view of reality is conditioned by our position in space and time—not by our personalities, as we like to think." Space and time modify thought, affect a person's view of life. "Two paces west and the whole picture is changed."

Justine, the first novel of the *Quartet,* opens with a description of Alexandria and a statement of its influence on the people who live in it.

> . . . what is this city of ours? What is resumed in the word Alexandria? . . . a thousand dust-tormented streets. . . . I remember Nessim once saying . . . that Alexandria was the great wine-press of love; those who emerged from it were

the sick men, the solitaries, the prophets—I mean all who have been deeply wounded in their sex. . . .

Streets that run back from the docks with their tattered rotten supercargo of houses, breathing into each other's mouths, keeling over. Shuttered balconies swarming with rats, and old women whose hair is full of the blood of ticks. . . . The black ribbon of flies attaching itself to the lips and eyes of the children. . . . The sores like ponds—the incubation of a human misery of such proportions that one was aghast, and all one's human feelings overflowed into disgust and terror.

I wished I could imitate the self-confident directness with which Justine threaded her way through these streets toward the cafe where I waited for her. . . .

Justine's view of life has been conditioned by the city. She has "emerged" from Alexandria, "the great wine press of love . . . deeply wounded." In one of her various responses to sex, she says to her lover, "Quick, *Engorge-moi.* From desire to revulsion—let's get it over." With more desire to untie "some unresolved inner knot" than to feel her lover physically or emotionally, Justine finds intimacy in the "flirtation of minds prematurely exhausted by experience."

Justine is the way she is because of *where* she is, because of the point-instant in which she lives. The setting of *The Alexandria Quartet,* the city of Alexandria, with its "hot pavements . . . inflaming the body through its light clothing," "influences by its position in space and time" the existence, the essential being, of its inhabitants.

When reading for setting, ask yourself how setting functions as a psychological influence to shape personality, how the people are a product, an outgrowth of their physical environment.

Setting as It Reveals Character

The way a character sees the setting may tell more about the character than it does about the actual setting. Here is how the artist-painter Gulley Jimson, the main character of Joyce Cary's *The Horse's Mouth,* sees his world as he walks along the Thames on an autumn day.

> Sun in a mist. Like an orange in a fried fish soup. All bright below. Low tide, dusty water and a crooked bar of straw, chicken boxes, dirt and oil from mud to mud. Like a viper swimming in skim milk.

Gulley transforms what to another person would be a bleak, commonplace autumn day into a splash of eccentric color. Only Gulley will see the Thames and its environs this way. With grizzled indifference to the "real" world, Gulley creates a higher order of reality. "Go love without the help of anything on earth; and that's real horse meat," Gulley says. The way Gulley Jimson sees his world is an index to his character. And it is Gulley's vision of life, his artistic imagination, that is the subject of the novel.

Setting as it reveals character is, in a way, the reverse of the preceding section, setting as it affects character. Gulley Jimson creates his environment; Justine is a product of hers. Gulley transforms his setting through his imagination; Justine is conditioned by hers.

Ask yourself whether character is affected or revealed by the setting in the work you are reading. Is the character a product of the environment, or is the environment a product of the character?

Setting as Background

The term "background," as used here, refers not to the events leading up to an action but to those things standing back, in the distance, beyond or behind the more conspicuous action in the foreground.

In drama, the term "setting" signifies, in its narrowest sense, the stage furnishings. But the stage furnishings or simply the objects standing behind the foreground action in a short story, novel, or poem may be the author's principal means of communicating the meaning and the emotion of his work.

Euripides' drama *The Trojan Women* presents the plight and lamentations of Trojan women after the fall of Troy. As the play opens, the walls of Troy stand smoldering far in the background—"in ruins . . . slowly burning, as yet more smoke than flame." In the foreground throughout the body of the play, Trojan women—waiting to be taken aboard Greek sailing ships, where they will pass into a life of slavery—grieve the fall of Troy. At the end of the play the walls of Troy flame and crash in the distance: Hecuba, the aged queen of Troy, speaks to other Trojan women:

A Woman.	Troy has perished, the great city. No city now, never again . . .
Hecuba.	O dwellings of the gods and O dear city, the spear came first and now only the red flame lives there . . .
A Woman.	The dust is rising, spreading out like a great wing of smoke . . .
Another.	The name has vanished from the land, and we are gone, one here, one there. And Troy is gone forever.
	(A great crash is heard.)
Hecuba.	Did you hear? . . .
A Woman.	The fall of Troy . . . Farewell, dear city. Farewell, my country, where once my children lived. On to the ships— There below, the Greek ships wait.

The walls of Troy emphasize and symbolize the present and future grief, pain, and suffering—the past glory and greatness of Troy and her people. This piece of stage setting far in the background states the subject and theme of the play as much as do the actions and the dialogue of the characters in the foreground. The foremost subject of the play, the fall of Troy and all it signifies, stands in the background.

The background of a poem, play, or story, then, may interact with the action in the foreground, providing harmony or contrast. A mountain, a gate, a wall, though standing undramatically in the distance, may be a clue to the meaning of the total work.

When reading for setting, notice the background for the action and ask yourself how that background complements or sets off what goes on in the foreground.

Setting as a State of Mind

Setting not only may represent an actual, physical place in the world but also may be an equivalent for a mental-emotional condition of an author, narrator, or character. In William Butler Yeats's poem "Sailing to Byzantium," Byzantium refers to the ancient capital of the Eastern Roman Empire, seat of Greek Orthodox Christianity. However, within the context of the poem, Byzantium "means" something on a very different level from a geographical place on the map. The poet begins by telling us that the sensual world of youth is no place for old men, that in that "dying" world "all neglect/Monuments of unaging intellect," and that an old man is "a paltry thing,/A tattered coat upon a stick, unless/Soul clap its hands and sing. . . ." But here in this physical world there is no "singing school" for the soul. Therefore, the poet has sailed to Byzantium, a place where the soul of an aged man may learn to sing. And the poet addresses "sages" in a mosaic; that is, the figures of colored glass inlaid in a wall:

> O sages standing in God's holy fire
> As in the gold mosaic of a wall,
> Come from the holy fire, perne in a gyre,
> And be the singing-masters of my soul.

The sages represent the soul that the poet finds in art, in creativity, in imagination. Here in Byzantium, "out of nature," out of the physical world of the young or the paltry old, he will learn to take

> . . . such a form as Grecian goldsmiths make
> Of hammered gold and gold enameling
> To keep a drowsy Emperor awake,
> Or set upon a golden bough to sing
> To lords and ladies of Byzantium
> Of what is past, or passing, or to come.

Within the context of the poem, then, Byzantium is not so much a place that once existed in the Bosphorus in Asia Minor as it is the poetic expression formulated in the poem itself—an internal place where the poet may attain a high degree of artistic and spiritual development. In Byzantium the poet would free himself from the physical, mortal world and become one with a spiritual, immortal world.

Setting, then, may function within a work in different but related ways; it may cause action, affect character, reveal character, serve as background, and stand for a state of mind. Ask yourself how setting and plot interact, how character relates to setting, and what the psychological as well as the physical meanings of setting are.

Reading Techniques

Most of us read for the action of a story. We are tempted to skim over long descriptive passages. In a literary work of quality, however, setting does more than inform the reader of the where and when of the story. The two techniques given below can help a reader become aware of the larger implications of setting. The first technique suggests two ways of distinguishing abstract statements and concrete details when both are given. The second technique illustrates methods for tracing possible abstract correlations of setting when only the concrete details are given.

Outlining and Marking to Distinguish Abstract Statements and Concrete Details

Setting is usually a description of a number of objects. But objects have meaning. Sometimes an author will simply present the objects, leaving their meaning to the inferences of the reader. At other times an author will make an abstract statement which explicitly reveals the meaning of the objects; that is, the author will generalize about them. It is useful to distinguish abstract statements about the setting from the concrete details of the setting.

In the opening pages of *Père Goriot* Honoré de Balzac describes the Parisian boarding-house Maison Vauquer.

> The drawing-room presented a forlorn and melancholoy appearance: the old horse-hair furniture, ragged and worn; the floor uneven and out of repair; the walls, paneled with varnished paper . . . the stone chimneypiece, where the fire was always laid and never lighted, and where a dismal clock in blue marble was flanked and supported on either side by vases of old, dusty, artificial flowers—all produced a chilling and depressing effect, which was in no wise counteracted by the odor which always pervaded the room: an odor which is like nothing else, a conglomeration of accumulated smells which can only be described by the words "boarding-house odor."

The paragraph is a combination of abstract statement (generalizations about things, the objects) and concrete detail (the objects, the things themselves). The method given below for clarifying the abstract and concrete suggests, or at least is not unlike, the mental process of the author when he wrote the paragraph.

	Concrete Details		Abstract Statements
furniture	——————	ragged and worn	
floor	——————	uneven	
walls	——————	varnished paper	(1) *a forlorn and melancholy appearance*
chimney-piece	——————	fire never lighted	
clock	——————	blue marble	(2) *a chilling and depressing effect*
vases	——————	dusty, artificial flowers	
odor	——————	boarding-house conglomeration of accumulated smells	

Abstract statements most often occur at the beginning or end of a paragraph. The concrete details which support, prove, or give evidence for the abstract statement most often comprise the body of the paragraph. Simply marking a paragraph for abstract statements and concrete details when both occur is one way of clarifying a passage. Balzac's description of the Maison Vauquer continues:

> But, dismal and unattractive as was this room, it was like a dainty and sweet-scented boudoir compared with the dining-room beyond. There the paint on the walls, indistinct at best, was ornamented by fantastic designs composed of the dirt which crusted it; there the sticky side-boards were adorned with old, empty bottles and piles of thick crockery from the manufactory at Tournay; there were assembled those indestructible articles of furniture which, once arrived at a certain point of decay, seem to survive all further attacks of age: invalid-chairs, wrteched little mats, always unraveling and never quite gone; Argand lamps, with dust and oil equally mixed; rusty old foot-stoves minus their hinges, horrible engravings framed in black wood, a long table covered with greasy oil-cloth—everything old, decaying, tottering, corroded with dirt and age, maimed and perishing. It was the reign of penurious and grasping misery without a gleam of poetry to lighten it.

{ abstract

{ abstract

In the first four pages of *Père Goriot* Balzac describes the section of Paris in which the Maison Vauquer is located. He then describes the Maison—from outside, from inside, room by room, from bottom to top. Only after this careful presentation of setting does a character appear on the scene. And then it may be noted that the character is as much setting as she is character. Here is Mme. Vauquer as she enters the dining room:

> ... a plump little woman, rapidly growing old, who was adorned with a tulle cap, from beneath which hung a curl of false hair. Her countenance was as fresh and sharp as the first frost of autumn; she had a plump face, from the

middle of which protruded a nose like a parrot's beak; her badly fitting slippers, her petticoat, between the rents of which little tufts of the wadded lining were sticking out; her whole appearance, in short, harmonized perfectly with the apartment in which she stood, and the mansion over which she presided. It was like the prison and the jailer—each was a part of the other. She was an epitome of the drawing-room, the dining-room, the kitchen, and—presumably—of the boarders also.

This description of Mme. Vauquer's physical appearance is as much setting as is the description of the Maison itself. The reader enters the world of *Père Goriot* through the setting, and the setting permeates everything in that world. By way of the details of setting, the reader is led into Balzac's re-creation of nineteenth-century Paris, which through its "penurious and grasping misery" grinds down its inhabitants and leaves them "maimed and perishing."

Diagramming and Outlining to Discover Abstract Correlations of Setting

Because a work of literature is a unit, because it is all of a piece, the elements within it can be related to one another. The more connections a reader makes between different details of a work, the greater his understanding. Diagramming is one way of clarifying relationships. Although diagramming can be misleading, (it may make faulty relationships, or force distantly related elements into unnaturally close relationship), if done with care it focuses attention on details and may uncover relationships that are essential to a full understanding of the story. William Faulkner's short story "A Rose for Emily" may serve as an example of the value of making connections.

Miss Emily Grierson is an aristocratic southern lady. Her father, when he was alive, had driven away her suitors. After his death Emily takes a "sweetheart," a Yankee construction worker, Homer Barron. Homer attempts to desert Miss Emily after their "courtship." But Miss Emily (there is "insanity in the family") buys rat poisoning, gives it to Homer, and sleeps with his body in a room "decked and furnished as for a bridal." Some years later, after Emily's death, the townspeople enter the room and find a strand of Emily's "iron-gray hair" on the pillow next to Homer's decayed body.

The action of the story is not complicated. The action, in fact, implies that the subject of the story is the perversions of one frustrated spinster. The setting suggests a much larger view of life than does the action. The following portion of a sentence from Faulkner's story describes the place of the action:

Only Miss Emily's house was left, lifting its stubborn and coquettish decay above the cotton wagons and the gasoline pumps—an eyesore among eyesores.

The implications of this description of Emily's house are many. Emily Grierson is like her house. And both Emily and her house are a link between past and present. Three words, perhaps, characterize the aristocratic southern tradition as it is presented in this story: stubborn, coquettish, and decadent. And it is these same words that are used to describe Emily's house.

By tracing the relationships that extend from house to woman to tradition to past, the reader may discover that the story is not so much about the psychosis of Emily Grierson as about the decadent past in conflict with the gross present.

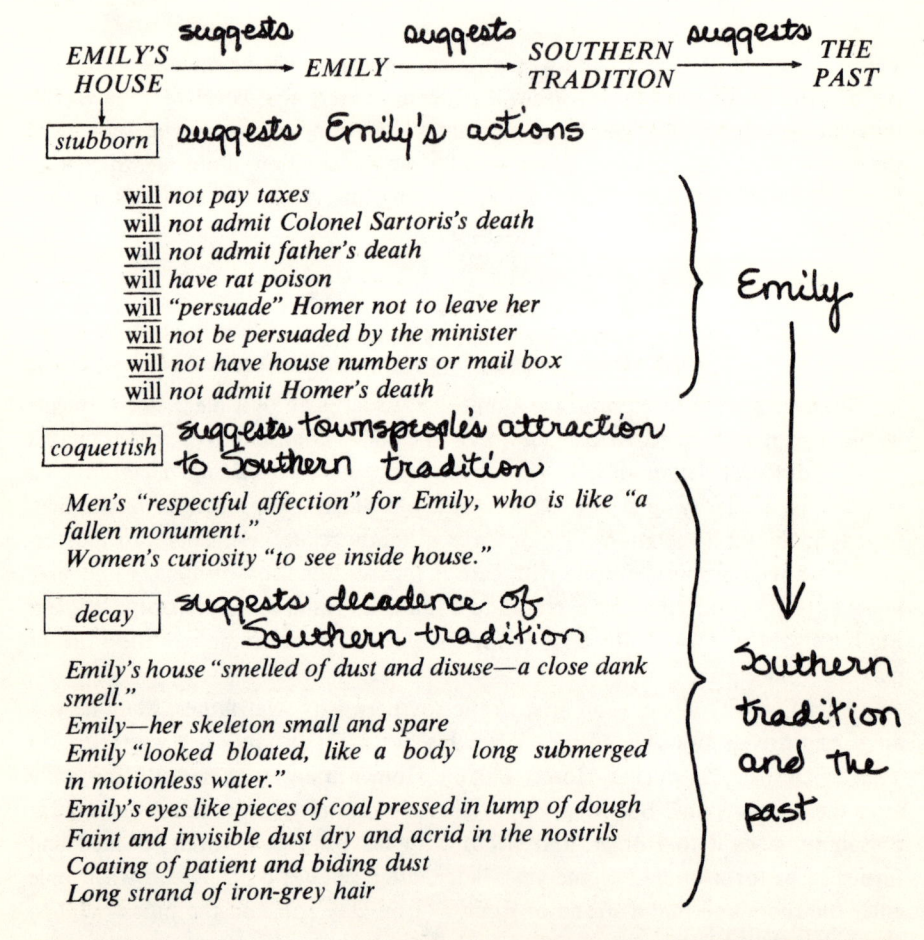

EMILY'S HOUSE —*suggests*→ EMILY —*suggests*→ SOUTHERN TRADITION —*suggests*→ THE PAST

[stubborn] *suggests Emily's actions*

- will not pay taxes
- will not admit Colonel Sartoris's death
- will not admit father's death
- will have rat poison
- will "persuade" Homer not to leave her
- will not be persuaded by the minister
- will not have house numbers or mail box
- will not admit Homer's death

} Emily

[coquettish] *suggests townspeople's attraction to Southern tradition*

Men's "respectful affection" for Emily, who is like "a fallen monument."
Women's curiosity "to see inside house."

[decay] *suggests decadence of Southern tradition*

Emily's house "smelled of dust and disuse—a close dank smell."
Emily—her skeleton small and spare
Emily "looked bloated, like a body long submerged in motionless water."
Emily's eyes like pieces of coal pressed in lump of dough
Faint and invisible dust dry and acrid in the nostrils
Coating of patient and biding dust
Long strand of iron-grey hair

} Southern tradition and the past

The idea of the story is emphasized through the apparent contrast (given in the description of the setting) between Emily's house and the gasoline pumps. The gasoline pumps below the stubborn decay of Emily's old house are, within the context of the story, associated with *Homer Barron*, who represents *Yankee materialism*, which, in turn, represents *the present*.

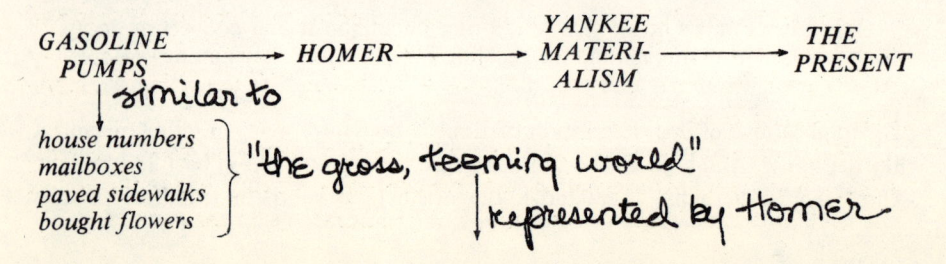

GASOLINE PUMPS —→ HOMER —→ YANKEE MATERIALISM —→ THE PRESENT

similar to

house numbers
mailboxes
paved sidewalks
bought flowers

} *"the gross, teeming world"*

represented by Homer

> *a big, dark ready man with a big voice and eyes lighter than his face*
> *the center of a lot of laughing*
> *a Northerner, a day laborer*
> *drank with the young men in the Elks' Club*
> *hat cocked and a cigar in his teeth*
> *profound and fleshless grin*

⎫ yankee materialism and the present

Diagrams like the ones shown here suggest a few possible relationships between setting and other elements in the story. If not followed rigidly, such outlines may provide a basis for a paper on the correlations of setting in "A Rose for Emily."

Writing Suggestions

A careful look at the details of the setting of a work may direct you to the story's larger meaning. The following questions focus attention on details and may uncover enough specific information to help you find a topic for a paper:

What time of day is it?—sunrise? sunset? . . .
What time of year is it?—spring? winter? . . .
What year or decade is it?—September 1, 1939? Roaring Twenties? . . .
Where does the action take place?—a mountain peak? a valley? . . .
What is the weather?—sunshine? a thunderstorm? . . .
What is the setting when the story begins? When it ends?—a Parisian garret? a deserted water hole? . . .
What is the setting when the high point in the action occurs?—a scaffold? a bedroom? . . .
Does the setting emphasize a psychological or spiritual state?—peace? anxiety? . . .
Is there a particular set of objects associated with a particular idea or emotion?—a dead cow and dead chickens? garbage disposal and power lawn mower? . . .
What are the characteristics of the setting—agricultural, static, and homogeneous? industrial, dynamic, and heterogeneous? . . .

When writing a paper on the function of setting in a story, you will need to do more than simply restate or describe the place and time of the action. Such a description may be a beginning, but you should go beyond this and show how setting is related to other aspects of the work.

To see how setting is related to other aspects, note the ways in which it functions within the work you are analyzing. Does setting (1) cause action, (2) affect character, (3) reveal character, (4) serve as important background for the action, (5) represent a state of mind?

You may, of course, write on only a part of the total setting—a street, a drawing room, a house: its psychological effect on the characters, its emphasis of the idea of the work, its symbolic function of suggesting meanings beyond those stated.

Point of View

4

POINT OF VIEW is a term used to describe the relation between an author and his story and between the author and the reader. Where is the storyteller in relation to the story? How much does he know about the action and the characters? How does he present his story to the reader? In what ways, if any, does the selected method of telling the story serve to intensify the overall emotional effect of the work?

A poem, short story, novel, or drama is by nature subjective or objective in respect to the degree of the author's participation. At the extremes of subjectivity and objectivity are the personal lyric poem and the stage play. In some, but not all, lyric poems the poet's relation to his material is immediate and apparent. The unconcealed lyric poet expresses directly a private feeling. William Butler Yeats walking along a London street "very homesick . . . heard a little trinkle of water and saw a fountain in a shop window . . . and began to remember" that he had planned "to live some day in a cottage on a little island called Innisfree"; and he wrote,

> I will arise and go now, and go to Innisfree,
> And a small cabin build there, of clay and wattles made:
> Nine bean-rows will I have there, a hive for the honeybee,
> And live alone in the bee-loud glade.

In a lyric in which a personal emotion of the author is given directly and not through an invented character, the author himself is felt as if present, "singing" his emotion in relation to one particular situation. In the drama, on the other hand, the author is concealed: Hamlet, Claudius, Horatio, Polonius, Ophelia . . . appear, act, and speak; Shakespeare remains out of sight. In the personal lyric the author is clearly visible; in the drama the author has, to as great an extent as is possible, disappeared.

When reading for point of view, you will be concerned primarily with the author's relation to his material, the degree to which the author is apparent in the work. Some authors—notably ones writing in this century—have felt it best to keep themselves hidden. James Joyce wrote,

> Ideally, the artist, like the God of Creation, remains within or behind or beyond or above his handiwork, invisible, refined out of existence, indifferent, paring his fingernails. . . . Subjectivity is a terrible thing. It is bad in this alone, that it reveals the authors' hands and feet.

But at the other extreme some authors have found it appropriate to show themselves. Thackeray in *Vanity Fair* steps forward and says,

> As we bring our characters forward, I will ask leave, as a man and a brother, not only to introduce them, but occasionally to step down from the platform, and talk about them: if they are good and kindly, to love them and shake them by the hand; if they are silly, to laugh at them confidentially in the reader's sleeve; if they are wicked and heartless, to abuse them in the strongest terms which politeness admits of.

Here are two extremes: Joyce advocating that the author be "invisible, refined out of existence" and Thackeray showing his hands and feet, laughing in the reader's sleeve.

Major Points of View in Narratives

A literary work seldom follows one of these two extremes of subjectivity or objectivity. Between these two extremes many points of view are open to the author. The **omniscient**, the **third-person-limited**, and the **first-person** are terms used to describe the three major ways of telling a short story or a novel. No two stories use any of these three methods in exactly the same way, but every story conforms to some degree to one of the three.

Omniscient

The **omniscient author allows himself the freedom of knowing everything.** The author can be felt hovering above his story, dropping down from time to time to reveal this character's emotions and that character's thoughts, stepping forward himself to comment on any or all of the characters or on the total action of the story. Not restricting himself to an external view of his characters, the omniscient author is free to tell their inner, hidden thoughts and emotions. He knows, in fact, more about what goes on inside his characters than they know themselves.

In *War and Peace* Tolstoy presents, before the vast panorama of Napoleon's invasion and retreat from Russia, a host of characters in a multitude of emotional states. Here is the author disclosing the emotions of the beautiful young Natasha on her way to her first grand ball:

> In the damp chill air and crowded closeness of the swaying carriage, she for the first time vividly imagined what was in store for her there at the hall, in those brightly lighted rooms—with music, flowers, dances, the Emperor, and all the brilliant young people of Petersburg. The prospect was so splendid that she hardly believed it would come true, so out of keeping was it with the chill darkness and closeness of the carriage.

And here is Tolstoy describing the emotions of Napoleon after the useless slaughter at the battle of Borodino:

> Napoleon . . . felt in his own person the sufferings and death he had witnessed on the battlefield. The heaviness of his head and chest reminded him of the possibility of suffering and death for himself. At that moment he did not desire Moscow, or victory, or glory (what need had he for any more glory?). The one thing he wished for was rest, tranquillity, and freedom.

And here to explain the apparently incomprehensible series of mistakes which brought about Napoleon's defeat is the author himself, stating the historical philosophy of his novel:

> Napoleon, the man of genius, did this! But to say that he destroyed his army because he wished to, or because he was very stupid, would be as unjust as to say that he had brought his troops to Moscow because he wished to and because he was very clever and a genius.
> In both cases his personal activity, having no more force than the personal activity of any soldier, merely coincided with the laws that guided the event.

And here is the author peering into the inner emotions of Pierre, who, having lived the life of a rich aristocrat, is captured by the French and in prison discovers for the first time the real values of life:

> Pierre felt a new joy and strength in life such as he had never before known. And this not only stayed with him during the whole of his imprisonment, but

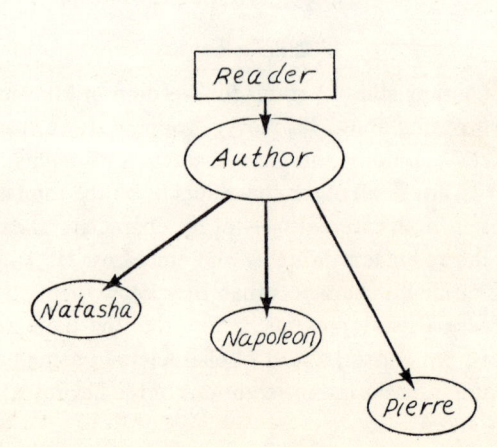

Figure 5 Omniscient Point of View

even grew in strength as the hardships of his position increased. . . . The absence of suffering, the satisfaction of one's needs and consequent freedom in the choice of one's occupation, that is, of one's way of life, now seemed to Pierre to be indubitably man's highest happiness.

Figure 5 is a drawing of the omniscient point of view. Here the reader knows everything because the author knows everything and tells him everything.

Third-Person-Limited

There are many variations on narratives given in the third person, and many terms have been used to describe the subtle variations of this viewpoint. The third-person-limited point of view is, perhaps, the most common of these variations. Understanding of it is a basis for understanding all other narratives using third-person pronouns.

The third-person-limited narrator selects a fixed point of consciousness within one person. Not allowing himself the freedom of moving about and looking into the minds of many characters, a narrator may place himself behind one character and confine himself to a knowledge of what this one character sees, hears, thinks, and feels.

In Katherine Mansfield's "Bliss," the narrator's point of consciousness is established in Bertha Young. The narrator knows Bertha's emotions as she turns a corner on her way home:

What can you do if you are thirty and, turning the corner of your own street, you are overcome, suddenly, by a feeling of bliss—absolute bliss!—as though you'd suddenly swallowed a bright piece of that late afternoon sun and it burned in your bosom, sending out a little shower of sparks into every particle, into every finger and toe?

Entering Bertha's house with her, the narrator knows what she thinks:

. . . How idiotic civilization is: Why be given a body if you have to keep it shut up in a case like a rare, rare fiddle?
"No, that about the fiddle is not quite what I mean," she thought, running up the steps . . .

The narrator knows how she feels as she throws off her coat in the dining room.

But in her bosom there was still that bright glowing place—that shower of little sparks coming from it. It was almost unbearable. She hardly dared to breathe for fear of fanning it higher, and yet she breathed deeply, deeply. She hardly dared to look into the cold mirror—but she did look, and it gave her back a woman, radiant, with smiling, trembling lips, with big, dark eyes and an air of listening, waiting for something . . . divine to happen . . .

The narrator knows what Bertha imagines about her relation with her husband and what she thinks about their friends as she waits for them to arrive for a dinner party she is giving.

> Harry and she were as much in love as ever, and they got on together splendidly and were really good pals. . . . And friends—modern, thrilling friends, writers and painters and poets or people keen on social questions—just the kind of friends they wanted.

But the narrator does not know everything, does not know what goes on inside the other characters—but knows only as much as Bertha sees or hears or thinks about them. Bertha hears one of her guests, the poet Eddie Warren, say

> "I *wonder* if you have seen Bilks' *new* poem called *Table d'Hôte* . . . It begins with an *incredibly* beautiful line: 'Why Must it Always be Tomato Soup?'"

The narrator sees only what Bertha can see:

> Bertha . . . turned her head towards the hall. And she saw . . . Harry with Miss Fulton's coat in his arms and Miss Fulton with her back turned to him and her head bent. He tossed the coat away, put his hands on her shoulders and turned her violently to him. His lips said: "I adore you," and Miss Fulton laid her moonbeam fingers on his cheeks and smiled her sleepy smile.

The emotional impact of "Bliss" lies in Mansfield's use of the third-person-limited point of view. The reader, as it were, stands behind the narrator as the narrator stands behind Bertha. Reader and narrator know what Bertha thinks about her life. But there is (or should be) a gap between what Bertha thinks about her life and what the reader thinks about it. Bertha thinks she feels "absolute bliss." As the story progresses, however, the reader comes to see that she is not feeling bliss—not real bliss—at all; instead, she is displaying an extreme form of self-deception. Similarly, Bertha may think that the poet, Eddie Warren, is a "thrilling" friend; but the reader (though he sees only as much of Eddie as Bertha does) thinks differently.

The third-person-limited point of view is effective because of this gap that may exist between the character's awareness and the reader's awareness. By way of this gap, the author is able to reveal not only the thoughts and feelings of a character, but the total state of the character's consciousness.

Figure 6 is a drawing of the third-person-limited point of view. Here the reader and the author are confined to a knowledge of what Bertha sees, hears, thinks, and feels—but reader and author think very differently about these things than Bertha does.

Figure 6   Third-Person-Limited Point of View

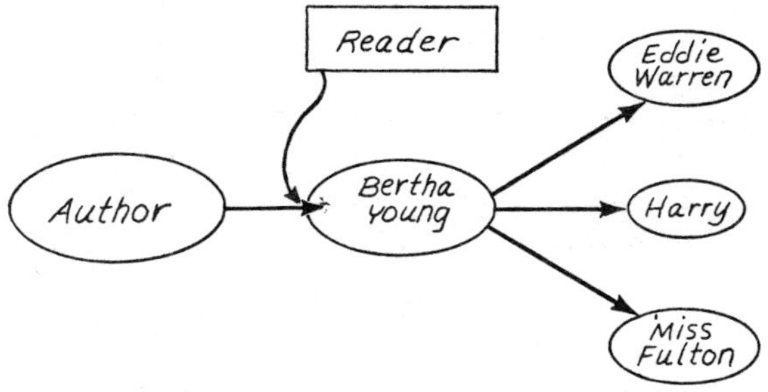

First-Person

An author may exclude himself from his story or novel by **letting a character within the story tell the story in the first person.** The first-person narrator is free to tell his own thoughts and feelings. But he is unable to look into the minds of other people; he can only guess what goes on there. All that is seen, heard, and thought is determined by the experience of the narrating "I." All that is seen is seen through his mentality.

Not Mark Twain, not a third-person narrator, but Huck Finn himself tells the *Adventures of Huckleberry Finn.* The reader knows Huck, Tom Sawyer, Jim, the Widow Douglas, and the other characters only through the eyes and mind of Huck Finn. Here is Huck describing an evening with his father in a cabin in the woods:

> After supper pap took the jug, and said he had enough whiskey there for two drunks and one delirium tremens. That was always his word. I judged he would be blind drunk in about an hour. . . . He drank, and drank, and tumbled down on his blankets. . . .
>
> I don't know how long I was asleep, but all of a sudden there was an awful scream and I was up. There was pap, looking wild and skipping around every which way and yelling about snakes. He said they was crawling up his legs; and then he would give a jump and scream, and say one had bit him on the cheek—but I couldn't see no snakes. He started and run round and round the cabin, hollering "take him off! take him off! he's biting me on the neck!" I never see a man look so wild in the eyes. Pretty soon he was all fagged out, and fell down panting; then rolling over and over, wonderful fast, kicking things every which way, and striking and grabbing at the air with his hands, and screaming, and saying there was devils ahold of him. He wore out, by-and-by, and laid still a while, moaning. Then he laid stiller, and didn't make a sound. I could hear the owls and the wolves, away off in the woods, and it seemed terrible still.

In the first-person point of view, as in the third-person-limited, there may be a gap between reader and character. The reader stands above Huck's description of pap's "awful scream" and pap's rolling over "wonderful fast" and Huck's hearing "the owls and the wolves, away off in the woods, and it seemed terrible still." Older and less innocent than the narrating "I," the reader sees more of Huck's goodness and innocence, and more of the violence and meanness of the world that surrounds Huck, than Huck sees himself. Figure 7 is a drawing of the first-person point of view. Here the author stays out of sight. He creates Huck and lets Huck stand by himself and tell his own story. The reader hears only what Huck says. But the reader's understanding of what Huck says about his world is larger than is Huck's understanding of it.

Figure 7   First-Person Point of View

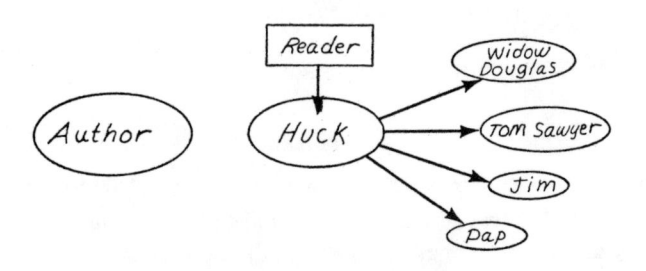

Stream of Consciousness

A variation of the first-person point of view, stream of consciousness is **a literary technique in which the author records what goes on in the mind of a character.** Like the first-person narrator, the stream-of-consciousness character is in the literary work. And, as with the first-person narrative, the author of the stream-of-consciousness technique is out of sight. Unlike the first-person narrator, the stream-of-consciousness character does not speak or write his story but is revealed through the rendering of the inner flow of his thought. The author of the stream-of-consciousness technique does not rearrange the mental activities of his character into a logical, sensible pattern but, instead, presents the flow of thought as it moves by way of free association from subject to subject. Here is an example of the associative wanderings of the musings of Leopold Bloom in James Joyce's *Ulysses:*

> Imagine trying to eat tripe and cowheel. Where was the chap I saw in that picture somewhere? Oh, in the dead sea, floating, on his back, reading a book with a parasol open. Couldn't sink if you tried: so thick with salt. Because the weight of the water, no, the weight of the body in the water is equal to the weight of the. Or is it the volume is equal to the weight? It's a law something like that. Vance in high school cracking his fingerjoints, teaching. The college curriculum. Cracking curriculum. . . .

The author makes known the hidden, inner world of Bloom's existence by showing us not only what Bloom thinks but the way his mind works as he thinks it. The reader can only guess how Bloom's mind gets from one subject to another. Thinking of eating tripe may have conjured up the image of something bloated; and this image of something bloated calls to mind a picture he once saw of a man afloat in the Dead Sea; and this, in turn, brings to mind a forgotten law of hydrostatics—which he gives over trying to remember as this thought is replaced by the auditory image of the teacher in the classroom (who may have disturbed him while he was trying to understand the law) cracking his knuckles; and this, in turn, is the basis for the pun "cracking curriculum."

If, as has been said, we are what we think but not what we think we are, then the stream-of-consciousness technique is a penetrating revelation of the inner man. From the few lines quoted above, the reader is given insights into the history, emotions, and character of Leopold Bloom. Figure 8 is a drawing of the stream-of-consciousness technique. Here the author is out of sight. He does not comment on or intrude on the character's flow of thoughts. The reader sees only what goes on in the character's mind. But the reader's understanding of what goes on in the character's mind may be different from the character's understanding of it. The character himself may not be aware of how his mind works or even be conscious of what he is thinking.

Figure 8 Stream-of-Consciousness Technique

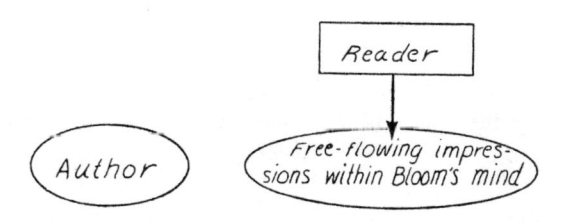

Reading Techniques: Diagramming and Outlining Point of View

Point of view is sometimes the key to an understanding of a literary work. But (and this is especially so in modern literature) the way an author presents his story to the reader can be both subtle and intricate. Sometimes a diagram or an outline will throw light on an author's handling of point of view.

Joseph Conrad's complex use of viewpoint in *Heart of Darkness* may easily be overlooked. Yet to a great extent the reader's experience of this story lies in his awareness of the author's relation to him. How does Conrad tell his story? What techniques does he use to keep himself out of sight?

Heart of Darkness is about a Mr. Kurtz, a European who went into the Belgian Congo as "an emissary of pity and science, and progress" to bring "light" to the natives. Once in the Congo, however, Kurtz (overwhelmed by the wilderness "which seemed to draw him to its pitiless breast by the awakening of forgotten and brutal instincts") gratifies his "monstrous passions" by committing atrocities against the natives.

But *Heart of Darkness* is more than a story about Kurtz. It is also a story about the effect of Kurtz's experience on *two* first-person narrators.

An unnamed narrator opens the story. Five men (one of them the unnamed first narrator and one of them the man who is to become the second narrator) are on a cruising yawl anchored in the Thames, waiting for the tide to turn. The first narrator describes the Thames and remembers the "greatness" that had "floated on the ebb of that river."

Then the second narrator, an old seaman named Marlow, begins one of his "inconclusive tales" and becomes the principal narrator of the story that follows. As Marlow opens his tale about Kurtz, he says, "to understand the effect of it on me you ought to know . . . how I went up that river to the place where I met the poor chap. . . . It was the culminating point of my experience." The first narrator and the other three men aboard the yawl now listen to Marlow tell of the effect of Kurtz's experience on him.

Marlow tells how he once went up a long river in a battered old steamboat, how he met Kurtz at a distant outpost in the heart of Africa, and how he heard Kurtz's pronouncement "upon the adventures of his soul on this earth." Kurtz dies, his body is buried in a muddy hole, and Marlow returns to Europe with a packet of Kurtz's letters to deliver to Kurtz's fianceé. Marlow delivers the packet, tells the financeé a lie about Kurtz's last words and is affected by the lie he tells to the extent that it seems as if his heart will stand still.

Marlow's tale is finished; the tide has turned. The first narrator (on the cruising yawl with the other three men who have been listening to Marlow's tale) looks out to sea, where the "tranquil waterway leading to the uttermost ends of the earth flowed sombre under an overcast sky—seemed to lead into the heart of an immense darkness."

Thus, we, the readers, hear an unnamed narrator tell us the story he once heard an old seaman, Marlow, tell him about his, Marlow's, experience of Kurtz's experience in Africa. Of the four listeners, perhaps only the first narrator understands the effect of Kurtz's experience on Marlow and is similarly affected.

But Kurtz's experience is not only Marlow's and the first narrator's but, by extension, the reader's. About *Heart of Darkness* Conrad wrote that it is a "record of experience" written with the "purpose of bringing home to the minds and bosoms of the readers . . . that sombre theme. . . ." The total effect of *Heart of Darkness* is aimed at the reader, and this effect Conrad rendered in large part through his use of double first-person narrators. Sketching the point of view of *Heart of Darkness* is the beginning of an understanding of the story (see Figure 9).

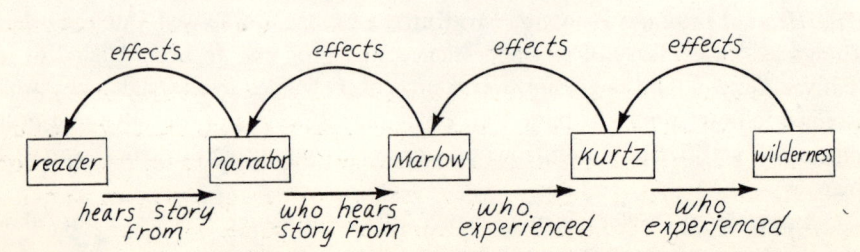

Figure 9 Point of View *of* Heart of Darkness

An outline of these interrelating effects, with quotes as supporting evidence, might look like this:

Effect *of the wilderness on Kurtz*
> Marlow: "*I think the knowledge of Kurtz's deficiency came to him at last.* . . . *I think it* [*the wilderness*] *had whispered to him things about himself which he did not know.* . . ."
>
> *Kurtz's whisper of self-knowledge:* "*The horror! The horror!*"

Effect *of Kurtz's experience on Marlow*
> Marlow: "*Destiny. My destiny! Droll thing life is—that mysterious arrangement of merciless logic for a futile purpose. The most you can hope from it is some knowledge of yourself.* . . . *And it is not my own extremity I remember best—* . . . *No! It is his extremity that I seemed to have lived through.*"
>
> Marlow: "*I was within a hair's-breadth of the last opportunity for pronouncement, and I found with humiliation that probably I would have nothing to say.* . . . *Better his cry—much better. It was an affirmation, a moral victory.* . . ."

Effect *of Kurtz's and Marlow's experience on first narrator*
> Before *Marlow's tale, the first narrator evokes* "*the great spirit of the past upon the lower reaches of the Thames* . . . *what greatness had not floated on the ebb of that river.* . . ."
>
> After *Marlow's tale the first narrator says that the waterway of the Thames* "*seemed to lead into the heart of an immense darkness.*"

Effect *of Kurtz's and Marlow's and the first narrator's experience on the reader:*
> By implication the men aboard the cruising yawl listening to Marlow's tale represent the person reading the story. To these men Marlow says: "*This is the worst of trying to tell.* . . . *Here you all are* . . . *temperatures normal.* . . . *How can you imagine what particular region of the first ages a man's untrammeled feet may take him.* . . ."

We the readers, we with normal temperatures, if we have understood what Marlow has been "trying to tell," may also be affected as the first narrator was—though we too, like Marlow, may never attain to Kurtz's moment of self-knowledge; for we have not been directly affected by the wilderness, have not found that we lack all restraint, and have not glimpsed the inroads one's innermost self may make into the "heart of an immense darkness."

The reading techniques illustrated above are, of course, peculiar to *Heart of Darkness*. Conrad's "purpose" required a special point of view for its expression. Each story you analyze will require its own reading technique. But making the effort to work out a technique of your own for the point of view of a complex story is a means of clarifying difficult stories in preparation for a paper on them.

Writing Suggestions

Before you begin the actual writing of a paper on point of view, you will need to know where the author is in relation to his work and where he is in relation to the reader. Here are some questions which may give you a starting point.

How do we, the readers, know what goes on in a character's inner world—his moods and thoughts?—author tells us he had two distinct spiritual conditions? the character says, "I prefer not"? . . .

Does the author require us to make our own interpretations?—we see the little old lady rush out of her house and we hear her growl? we hear the man let out a little suppressed wheezing sound? . . .

Do we know only what one character knows but have greater insights into what he knows than he does?—the character lives a life of compromise but doesn't know it? a character fancies himself a great artist, but we have seen his art work? . . .

Is the narrator a character in the story? What kind of a person is he?—an abstainer fond of work? an inebriated loafer? . . .

What is the effect on the narrator of the story he tells?—as a middle-aged man he remembers when his mother rocked him in her arms and painfully realizes why he is the way he is? through trying to help the main character, the narrator also realizes that the universe has no meaning? . . .

Does the action take place inside a character's mind?—"and how he kissed me under the moorish wall . . . and then I asked him with my eyes to ask again yes"? . . .

Such questions will help to determine which of the basic points of view or variations on them the author has used: (1) the omniscient point of view—does he know everything, the thoughts and feelings, internal workings of many different people in many different places? (2) the third-person-limited—does he remain with one character, follow him about, know only what goes on inside this one character and see only as much as this one character sees? (3) first-person—is the storyteller a character in the story, telling the story as he knows it?

More than describing the point of view your author uses, you will need to show what special effects have been achieved by his use of it. By focusing on one incident—the climax, perhaps, or the consciousness of the main character—and showing how the emotional effect of the story has been intensified through the special use of point of view in respect to this one incident or character, you may find a topic for your paper.

Style

5

All writers have a **STYLE—an individual way of putting thoughts into words, a distinctive way of handling language.** As the impress on paper of the lines and whorls of an inked finger identify a man, so word choice and sentence structure characterize an author.

Because of the uniqueness of every man's style, even a skilled translator, who attempts to transfer as faithfully as possible the qualities of a work of literature into another language, is unable to capture exactly the meaning and the emotion of the original. Following are a passage from Chaucer's *The Canterbury Tales* and two translations of the same passage. The original was written in Middle English in about A.D. 1390; the two translations were written in Modern English in this century. In the passage quoted, the Wife of Bath, one of the characters in *The Canterbury Tales,* comments on her past life. The "Goodwife"—gap-toothed, face red and bold, short skirt about her broad hips, tight scarlet hose—knows the old art of love, which she practiced generously during her youth. Astride an ambling horse on a pilgrimage to Canterbury, she tells her fellow pilgrims:

> But, Lord Crist! whan that it remembreth me
> Upon my yowthe, and on my jolitee,
> It tikleth me aboute myn herte roote.
> Unto this day it dooth myn herte boote
> That I have had my world as in my tyme.
> But age, allas! that al wol envenyme,
> Hath me biraft my beautee and my pith.
> Lat go, farewell, the devel go there with.
>
> (Chaucer)

But Lord, Lord! when I mind me of my youth and mirth, it tickles me about the root of my heart! To this very day it does my heart good that I have had my fling in my time. But alas! age, that envenoms all things, has bereft me of my pith and my beauty. Let them go. Farewell! the Devil go with them.

(Tatlock and MacKaye translation)

> But Lord Christ! When I do remember me
> Upon my youth and on my jollity,
> It tickles me about my heart's deep root.
> To this day does my heart sing in salute
> That I have had my world in my own time.
> But age, alas! That poisons every prime,
> Has taken away my beauty and my pith;
> Let go, farewell, the devil go therewith!
> (J.U. Nicholson translation)

Though Chaucer's language is very similar to Modern English, the effect of sound, word choice, and sentence structure distinguishes the original from the translations. Also, the translations differ from each other. All three passages have a markedly distinct "feel" about them.

Your task in reading for style is to study an author's language carefully enough to gain a feeling for it. "Without a feeling for language," it has been said, "the reader remains half-blind and deaf to literature." But gaining a feeling for language can be a slow process, for it may require that you read as "deliberately" as the writer wrote. And good writers do not write as easily and effortlessly as most of us read. "Oh! What a rascal of a thing style is!" the novelist Flaubert said. "The language in itself is most painful to me." Maupassant, Flaubert's student, declared, "whatever the thing is that one wishes to say, there is one word to express it, one verb to animate it, and one adjective to qualify it. Therefore, one must search until one has found them, this word, this verb, this adjective."

Viewed in the simplest way, a work of literature is composed of words arranged into sentences. A study of style includes an examination of word choice and sentence structure; that is of **DICTION** and **SYNTAX**.

Diction

The quality of a writer's style depends on his diction; that is, on **the way the author selects and arranges words.** The quality of the words themselves depends on their *meaning* and their *sound*.

Meaning

A literary artist may select a word not only for **the specific meaning, for the express definition of the word**—that is, for its **DENOTATION**; but also for **the related implications, for the emotional associations that accompany a word**—that is, for its **CONNOTATIONS.** As the emotional effect of a *work* of literature depends to a large extent on what is left unsaid, so the emotional effect of a *word* of that literature, the smallest unit of composition, often depends not only on the thing designated by the word but also on what is suggested. Because a word may be charged with multiple meanings, it is especially important that you, the reader, be sensitive to its connotations.

In George Herbert's poem "The Collar," for example, the word "collar" has a number of meanings. In a cry of petulant emotion the poet rebels against the restraints of canon law ("No more;/I will abroad!/What? shall I ever sigh and pine?"), only to be startled back to God's law when he hears the Lord speak ("Methought I heard one calling, *Child!*/ And I replied, *My Lord"*). Within the context of the poem the emotional associations of "collar" are many:

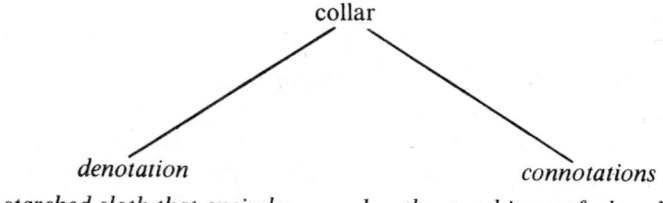

collar

denotation

starched cloth that encircles and fastens around the neck

connotations

1. the teachings of the church as they encircle and restrain and fasten the clergyman's private life
2. the life of the poet: restricted, limited, fearful of death, harnessed, burdened with the yoke of canon law
3. God's way of inner freedom, rest, and peace through spiritual restraint

Sound

As the reader looks for meaning, sound often goes unheard. And yet a word is sound with meaning, and the sound of a word may in itself—distinct from its denotation and connotations—be the author's chief means of communication. In the following passage from the Anna Livia Plurabella section of James Joyce's *Finnegans Wake*, sound is of primary importance. Read the passage aloud to sense its emotion.

> She was just a young thin pale soft shy slim slip of a thing then, sauntering, by silvamoonlake and he was a heavy trudging lurching lieabroad of a Curraghman, making his hay for whose sun to shine on, as tough as the oaktrees (peats be with them!) used to rustle that time down by the dykes of killing Kildare, for forstfellfoss with a plash across her.

To communicate emotion and emphasize meaning Joyce uses (1) alliteration, (2) assonance, (3) pun, and (4) onomatopoeia.

Alliteration is **the repetition of the same initial consonant sound in two or more words or in two or more syllables of a word.**

*s*oft, *s*ly, *s*lim, *s*lip, *s*auntering, *s*ilvamoonlake
*l*urching, *l*ieabroad
*h*is, *h*ay
*s*un, *s*hine
*d*own, *d*ykes
*k*illing, *K*ildare
*f*orst*f*ell*f*oss

Assonance is the similarity of vowel sounds but the dissimilarity of the succeeding consonant sounds in the stressed syllables of two or more words.

>sl*i*m, sl*i*p
>tr*u*dging, l*u*rching, C*u*rraghman

A **Pun** is the humorous use of a word which is similar in sound to another word with a different meaning.

>*lieabroad*
>*peats*

To understand a pun it is necessary to see the double meanings of the word. Perhaps Joyce is playing with words when he speaks of the Curraghman as a *lieabroad:* (1) *lie* meaning "to stretch out, extend oneself," *abroad* meaning "extensively in height and width"; (2) *lie* meaning "to lie with or to seduce," *a broad* meaning (the author relies on American slang for his pun) "a girl or woman."

The sound of "peats be with them" suggests "peace be with them." The oak trees have passed on to the other world: (1) peace be with them; (2) they have become peat, decayed plant matter.

Onomatopoeia is the formation of a word so that its sound is associated with its meaning.

>forstfell*foss* with a *plash* across her

The *foss* (the author may be punning here again) implies, perhaps, the way and the speed with which the trees fell. The *plash* intimates the sound they made when they fell across Anna, which, in turn, suggests the result of the Curraghman's influence and activities with Anna.

The whole passage is, in effect, onomatopoeia. The alliterative "s" consonant sounds, made in the front of the mouth, the monosyllabic *soft, shy, slim, slip,* and the polysyllabic *silvamoonlake* "mean" that Anna Livia is light, gay, carefree. The assonance of the throaty vowel sounds of *trudging* and *lurching,* made in the back of the mouth, are equivalents of the heavy Curraghman's nature. Sound communicates the presences of Anna and the Curraghman and makes audible their relationship. Sound thus functions as character delineation and narrative action, and serves as a vehicle for the serio-comic tone of the adventures of Anna Livia as "She thought she's sankh neathe the ground with nymphant shame when he [the Curraghman] gave her the tigris eye!" and "offon he jumpnad her." To a large extent the sound of the language of *Finnegans Wake* is its meaning.

There are more implications of the auditory effects of this passage than have been noted here. Of course, few of the passages you read will be as rich in sound as this one. But from what has been said it should be apparent to you that meaning is received, in part, from what is heard, and that the feeling of a passage of literature may be conveyed by the magic quality of the sound of its words.

Syntax

A writer's style, as has been noted, is indicated by his choice of words and by the way he puts those words together. Though the word is the smallest unit of composition, the sentence—a group of words expressing a complete thought—is often considered to be the most basic unit of composition and the backbone of a writer's style. When asked how he wrote, the modern novelist Philip Roth replied, "A sentence at a time." We walk not a foot at a time but a step at a time. We think in sentences and our sentences disclose the way we think. And it is partly for this reason that most writers take care with their sentences. Gertrude Stein, novelist and sometimes stylistic coach of the young Ernest Hemingway, said of her writing, "[I] ... was struggling with ... sentences, those long sentences that had to be so exactly carried out. Sentences not only words but sentences and always sentences have been ... [my] life long passion."

A sentence may be studied from different standpoints: in regard to its *form* (Is it simple, compound, complex?), its *function* (Is it declarative, interrogative, exclamatory, imperative?) its *construction* (Is it *loose, periodic, balanced?*). Most sentences are not simply loose, periodic, or balanced but a mixture of all three. Yet for the purpose of stylistic analysis it is helpful to know the essential nature of these three kinds of word arrangements.

The **Loose Sentence**[1] **states the main thought near the beginning of the sentence in an independent clause to which qualifying phrases and dependent and independent clauses may be added**, giving additional information and lengthening the sentence. Here is the first sentence of Daniel Defoe's *The Adventures of Robinson Crusoe:*

> I was born in the year 1632, in the city of York, of a good family, though not of that country, my father being a foreigner of Bremen, who settled first at Hull: he got a good estate by merchandise, and leaving off his trade, lived afterward at York, from whence he had married my mother, whose relations were named Robinson, a very good family in that country, and from whom I was called Robinson Kreutznoer; but, by the usual corruption of words in England, we are now called, nay, we call ourselves, and write our name Crusoe, and so my companions always called me.

The main thought is expressed in the independent clause "I was born in the year 1632." The sentence might have ended at this point, or after "York" or "family" or "country" or any of several other places. But it does not; and the author adds detail after detail, phrase after phrase, clause after clause, rhythmically, casually, reflectively, extending the sentence and the reader's knowledge of Robinson Crusoe.

The **Periodic Sentence**, the opposite of the loose sentence, **withholds, until near the end, the completion of the main thought.** Following is a sentence from Henry James's "The Real Thing."

---

[1] For a discussion of the "cumulative sentence," a modern form of the "loose sentence," see Francis Christensen, "A Generative Rhetoric of the Sentence,' *College Composition and Communication,* October 1963.

> When the porter's wife (she used to answer the housebell), announced "A gentleman and a lady, sir," I had, as I often had in those days—the wish being father to the thought—an immediate vision of sitters.

When studying a sentence for style, you may sometimes find it helpful to isolate the basic subject-verb-complement pattern by diagramming. "I really do not know, Gertrude Stein said, "that anything has ever been more exciting than diagramming sentences... I like the feeling the everlasting feeling of sentences as they diagram themselves." Few of us have such a passion for diagramming, but some simple laying out of the sentence so as to clarify its framework for yourself can be useful. An outline of the periodic sentence above might look like this:

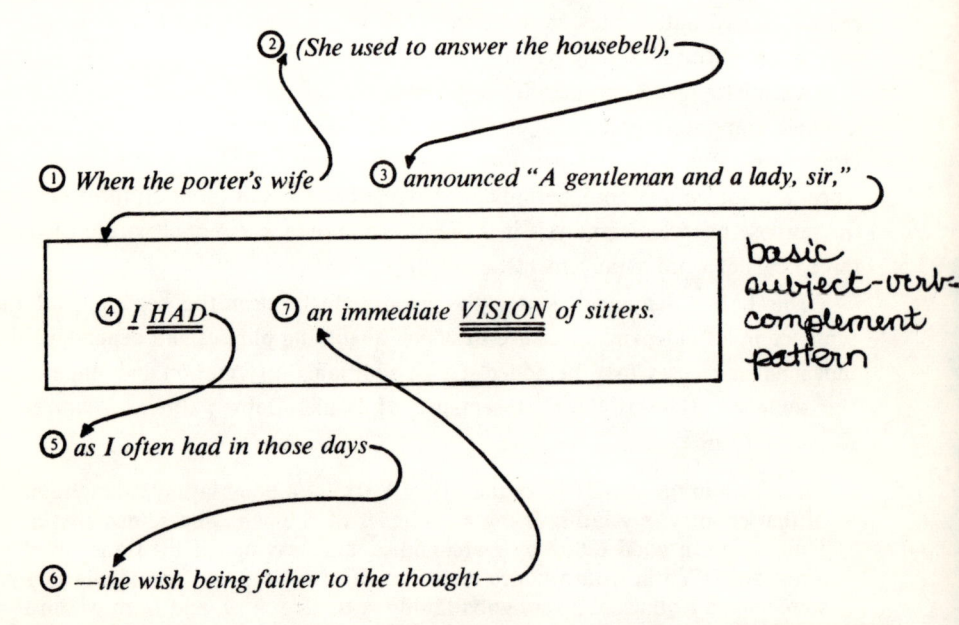

② *(She used to answer the housebell),*

① *When the porter's wife*   ③ *announced "A gentleman and a lady, sir,"*

④ <u>*I HAD*</u>   ⑦ *an immediate <u>VISION</u> of sitters.*

basic subject-verb-complement pattern

⑤ *as I often had in those days*

⑥ *—the wish being father to the thought—*

The reader is held in suspense by an introductory dependent clause [1] and [3] and a parenthetical clause [2], which precede the subject and verb [4]; he is further delayed by a conjunctive clause [5] and a gerund phrase [6], which follow the subject and verb, before arriving at the complement [7], "an immediate vision of sitters."

This periodic sentence characterizes the narrator who is the subject of the story. A paper might be written on the implications of each of the clauses and the emphasis placed on the word "vision." Such a study would include syntax, diction, and point of view to suggest the total meaning of "The Real Thing."

The Balanced Sentence presents similiar or antithetical ideas in parallel form. Elements of a sentence are united or disunited to emphasize likeness or unlikeness. The following lines from Alexander Pope's *An Essay on Man* are diagrammed to show parallelism (underscores) and antithesis (arrows). In these lines Pope uses parallelism and antithesis to express the possible harmony but essential disharmony of his subject, man, as he exists within a universe that is, in its completeness, perfect.

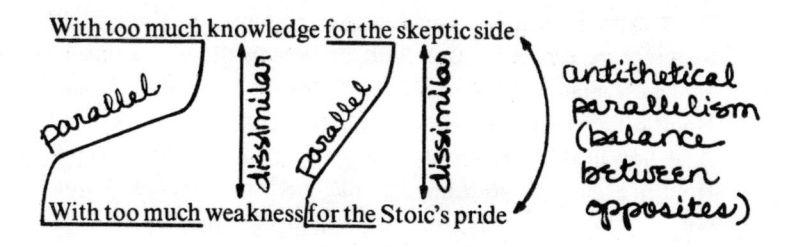

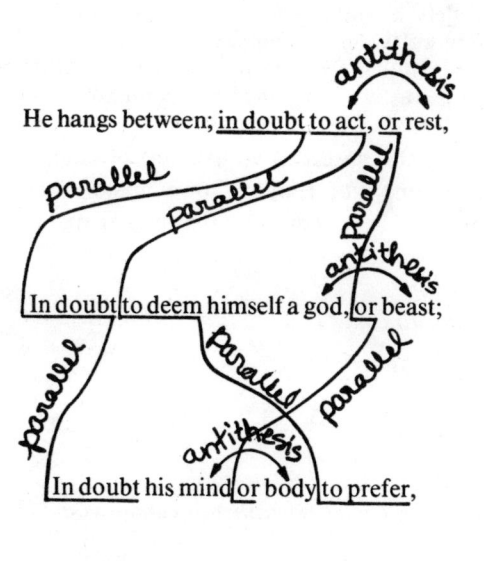

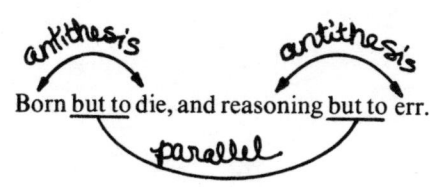

[Annotated diagram:]

With too much knowledge for the skeptic side
With too much weakness for the Stoic's pride

(parallel / dissimilar / parallel / dissimilar) — antithetical parallelism (balance between opposites)

He hangs between; in doubt to act, or rest,
In doubt to deem himself a god, or beast;
In doubt his mind or body to prefer,
Born but to die, and reasoning but to err.

[Annotations: parallel, antithesis]

It may be concluded that an author expresses himself, in part, by the way he arranges words and structures sentences. The use, modification, and mixing of loose, periodic, and balanced sentences is an indication of the way an author's mind works. Meaning is communicated not only by what is said but by the way it is said. The style of a sentence may tell as much as its contents.

Reading Techniques

Sometimes the meaning of a passage is not immediately apparent because of the way an author has put words together to form sentences. *Intense logical constructions* and *unusual syntactical constructions* are not uncommon, and they often need some untangling to help clarify meaning and disclose stylistic qualities.

Chapter Five

Intense logical constructions are common in the writings of many authors. Shakespeare especially was fond of having the characters in his plays speak in analytic syntax. In *Hamlet,* Hamlet, about to duel with Laertes, tells his friend Horatio that he will go ahead with the duel and will win but "thou wouldst not think how ill all's here about my heart." In an attempt to keep Hamlet from dueling, Horatio argues, "if your mind dislike anything, obey it! I will . . . say . . . you are not fit." Hamlet refutes Horatio's argument with

> Not a whit, we defy augury: there's a special providence in the fall of a sparrow. If it be now, 'tis not to come; if it be not to come, it will be now; if it be not now, yet it will come: the readiness is all: since no man has aught of what he leaves, what is't to leave betimes? Let be.

The second sentence of this speech is an example of compressed reasoning; more specifically, it is an example of Hamlet's own brand of mock logic. The image Hamlet uses in support of his argument is that of a sparrow in flight and the time (present or future) of the sparrow's fall from the sky:

If it be now, 'tis not to come

if now → *then not to come*

(If the sparrow's death comes now, then it cannot come in the future.)

if it be not to come, it will be now

then now > *if not to come*

(If the sparrow's death is not to come in the future, then it must come now.)

if it be not now, yet it will come

if not now → *then will come*

(If the sparrow's death does not come now, then it will come in the future.)

In addition to giving balance and symmetry to the logic through the parallelism of "if it be," the sentence illustrates the stylistic device of **DISJUNCTION**; that is, **the splitting of groups of words into two parts.** Because the main clause is preceded by a dependent conjunctive clause, each of the three logical alternatives of the time of the sparrow's fall is divided into two parts:

If it be now | *'tis not to come*
if it be not to come | *it will be now*
if it be not now | *yet it will come*

Note also that the syntax of the passage emphasizes character and plot. Reasoning in support of his going ahead with the duel, Hamlet likens man's death, and more directly his own death, to that of a sparrow's. Death will come—if not now, later. *When* does not matter. What does matter is that one be ready for it. The reader may sense that Hamlet, perhaps for the first time in the play (this would indicate a change, maybe even a reversal, in his emotions) is ready.

Unusual syntactical constructions which obscure the basic subject-verb-complement pattern of a sentence may be clarified by analysis. Breaking a sentence up into parts makes evident the function, relationship, and proportion of elements within the total construction.

In Shakespeare's *The Tempest* Prospero, a good man and wise magician who has ruled an enchanted island with justice, knows that the time has come for him to give up his magic arts, leave the island, and return to his native city of Milan, where "Every third thought shall be my grave." His work on the island nearly completed, Prospero, alone on stage, says,

Ye elves of hills, brooks, standing lakes and groves,
And ye that on the sands with printless foot
Do chase the ebbing Neptune and do fly him
When he comes back; you demi-puppets that
By moonshine do the green sour ringlets make,
Whereof the ewe not bites, and you whose pastime
Is to make midnight mushrooms, that rejoice
To hear the solemn curfew; by whose aid,
Weak masters though ye be, I have bedimm'd
The noontide sun, call'd forth the mutinous winds,
And 'twixt the green sea and the azured vault
Set roaring war: to the dread rattling thunder
Have I given fire and rifted Jove's stout oak
With his own bolt; the strong-based promontory
Have I made shake and by the spurs pluck'd up
The pine and cedar: graves at my command
Have waked their sleepers, oped, and let 'em forth
By my so potent art.

It has been said that "Shakespeare flies, we creep." The poet's brilliant flights may be more easily comprehended if they are first brought to earth by the method of analysis and then returned to flight for the full emotional experience of them. One way to expose the fine syntactical qualities of the above passage is to distinguish its major parts. Here is one possible diagram of the sentence:

54   Chapter Five

> *Ye elves of hills*
>   *brooks*
>   *lakes*
>   *groves*
>
> *ye that do chase . . .*
>   *do fly*
>
> *you demi-puppets that . . . ringlets make*
> *you whose pastime Is to make . . . mushrooms*

by whose aid (Weak masters though ye be)

> *I have* *bedimm'd . . . sun*
>   *call'd . . . winds*
>   *set . . . war*
>   *to . . . thunder Have I given fire*
>   *rifted oak*
>   *the . . . promontory Have I made shake*
>   *pluck'd up pine*
>   *cedar*
>   *graves Have waked sleepers*
>   *oped*
>   *let 'em forth*

by my so potent art

A — accretion of details (small, mysterious, dainty things)

points of contrast

B — accretion of details (large, amazing, powerful acts)

    The passage divides itself into two parts, which are fenced off from each other with the prepositional phrase "by whose aid." The phrase, besides its disjunctive service, functions as a connective between part A and part B to indicate their relationship. It is by the means or the agency of A that B is accomplished. Prospero is saying, "With the help of A, I have done B."

The sentence can be considered as a modification and combination of the three main kinds of stylistic sentences—periodic, loose, and balanced. The A part, a nominative of address, holds the reader in suspense by withholding completion of thought until part B—"I have bedimm'd the noontide sun." But after this possible completion of the thought, the speaker continues in part B to add detail after detail, example after example, until concluding with the prepositional phrase "by my so potent art."

In part A the "ye," "ye," "you," and "you" are parallel. In part B the verbs "bedimm'd," "call'd," and "set"; "given" and "rifted"; "made shake" and "pluck'd up"; "waked," "oped," and "let" are parallel. The two phrases "by whose aid" and "by my so potent art" are parallel and suggest that the "Weak masters" of part A are symbols or correlatives of Prospero's art.

The two-part division of the whole into A and B gives balance and symmetry to the sentence. It can be said that the main purpose of the syntax is to put into opposing points of emphasis the accretion of details in A with those in B. The elements of A refer to small, mysterious, dainty things; the elements of B refer to large, amazing, powerful acts.

A paper could be written on the magical qualities of the style of this passage and how it illustrates the character of Prospero, who is a harmonious and free will, a fully realized consciousness—which is the subject of *The Tempest,* considered to be Shakespeare's last complete play. If you understand the technique used to analyze the complex syntax of this sentence, you should be able to work through the syntax and to describe the stylistic qualities of almost any sentence.

Writing Suggestions

Do not attempt to analyze the style of a complete work, but select one representative passage. Before beginning to write, decide what aspect of style is outstanding or most interesting to you. By limiting your paper to a discussion of this one aspect and its implications, you will attain a workable focus while at the same time developing concrete evidence for a generalized statement about the whole work. Some things you might ask yourself are:

Are emotion and meaning communicated by sound?—heavy vowels? hissing consonants? . . .

What does the diction tell us about the speaker?—that she is a refined old lady? that he is a pompous ass? . . .

What sentence constructions does the author use to express himself?—periodic and stiff? loose and stringy? . . .

At what pace does the author speak?—leaps and flies? plods along methodically? . . .

In what proportion does the author use the abstract and concrete?—abhors

the abstract, prefers to speak of warts and chains? often uses the abstract, speaks of unseemly excretions and formidable bindings? . . .
How does the author present his story to the reader?—allows the reader's imagination full play? explains everything? . . .
In what ways does the style reveal the author's or speaker's emotional-mental outlook on life?—style is heavy, foggy, and involuted, suggesting a deep-seated gloom? style is lucid but crackles and jars, suggesting stringent gaiety? . . .
How does the style emphasize the meaning of the work?—simple words and simple sentence structure express the basic, primitive realities of life? large words and complex sentence structure express the majestic loftiness of metaphysical speculation? . . .

In a line, stanza, or passage, you might analyze the author's word choice by discussing the meaning of the words, both their denotation (their express definition) and their connotation (the emotional associations accompanying the words).

Or you may find that the sound of the words (alliteration, assonance, pun, onomatopeia) is of special significance.

Or perhaps you have discovered something interesting about the proportion of simple and complex sentences; of periodic, loose, or balanced sentences. Such studies may lead you to a statement concerning the general emotional effect exuding from the work.

Though an analysis of selected passages may comprise the body of your paper, you will also need to indicate how the style emphasizes larger meanings within the work.

Tone

6

TONE is the speaker's attitude, his relationship to, his feelings about his subject. In Owen Wister's *The Virginian,* Steve, one of the novel's "ungrammatical sons of the soil" says to the Virginian, "You're such a son-of-a-_____." The narrator, who is an Eastern dude unwise to the ways of "the sons of the sagebrush," comments:

> I had expected that the man would be struck down. He had used to the Virginian a term of heaviest insult, I thought. I had marvelled to hear it come so unheralded from Steve's friendly lips. And now I marvelled still more. Evidently he had meant no harm by it, and evidently no offence had been taken. Used thus, this language was plainly complimentary.

Later the Virginian is once again called, as Wister puts it, a "son-of-a-_____." But this time the words carry a different emotion, and the Virginian reacts accordingly. In a poker game with Trampas—tinhorn bronco-buster—the Virginian hesitates before betting:

> Therefore Trampas spoke. "Your bet, you son-of-a-_____." The Virginian's pistol came out, and his hand lay on the table, holding it unaimed. And as ever, the voice that sounded almost like a caress, but drawling a very little more than usual, so that there was almost a space between each word, he issued his orders to the man Trampas:—
> "When you call me that, *smile!*" And he looked at Trampas across the table.
> Yes, the voice was gentle. But in my ears it seemed as if somewhere the bell of death was ringing; and silence, like a stroke, fell on the large room. All men present, as if by some magnetic current, had become aware of this crisis. . . . I stood stock-still, and noticed various people crouching. . . .

Though the words they speak are the same, the Virginian accepts Steve's but not Trampas's. The *tone* in which the words were spoken has made the difference.

Trampas is ordered to "smile!"—that is, to give the words their proper coloration, the acceptable emotional meaning. Trampas's faulty tone and the Virginian's ear for it leaves the tinhorn bronco-buster with the uneasy alternative of having to "back down or draw his steel." Not only Trampas but the narrator and the crouching cowpunchers correctly interpret the *tone* of the Virginian's soft words, which carry with them the ring of a death bell.

Not only characters but authors speak in an individual tone of voice. An author necessarily has certain attitudes toward his subject; he reveals these attitudes by the way he tells his story. Conrad wrote that his *Heart of Darkness* "had to be given a sinister resonance, a tonality of its own, a continued vibration, that, I hoped, would hang in the air and dwell in the ear after the last note had been struck." The "sinister resonance" of *Heart of Darkness* arises from Conrad's attitude toward his subject; that is, his emotion for "the pure selfishness of European man when tackling the civilizing work in Africa." Because an author's attitude toward his subject is not always clear, you may not be able to arrive at exact conclusions about it. The author writes silent words on silent pages, and we, the readers, must try to perceive the tone of his voice.

Following are lines from Chaucer's *The Canterbury Tales* and T. S. Eliot's *The Waste Land*. The subject in both is April, but the two authors' attitudes toward the subject are very different. Chaucer opens his *Tales* with the life of April—its sweet showers that pierce the March drought to the root and will bring the plants to flower, its warm wind which inspires the tender shoots to growth, its young sun in the early part of its yearly course, its melody of small birds that are so moved by Nature that they sleep all night with open eyes, its people who then long to go on pilgrimages:

> Whan that Aprille with his shoures soote
> The droghte of March hath perced to the roote,
> And bathed every veyne in swich licour
> Of which vertu engendred is the flour;
> Whan Zephirus eek with his sweete breeth
> Inspired hath in every holt and heeth
> The tendre croppes, and the yonge sonne
> Hath in the Ram his halve cours yronne,
> And smale foweles maken melodye,
> That slepen al the nyght with open ye
> (So priketh hem nature in hir corages) ;
> Thanne longen folk to goon on pilgrimages.

Some five hundred years after Chaucer composed the above lines, T. S. Eliot wrote these opening lines to *The Waste Land:*

> April is the cruelest month, breeding
> Lilacs out of the dead land, mixing
> Memory and desire, stirring
> Dull roots with spring rain.

Both authors write of April. Both describe the cyclic movement of nature as it manifests itself in the spring of the year. Both speak of the growth of plants out of the land as a result of spring rain. But the emotion of the two poets in relation to their subject is markedly different. We as readers recognize the difference in emotion in these two passages by the effect on us of the quality of the words used; that is, by the effect on us of the difference in their tone.

The quality of Chaucer's words, their connotations, their emotional associations, suggest life—rich, gay, zestful, effusive:

> *shoures soote*—sweet, gentle, fresh, life-giving showers
> *licour*—moisture; rich, flavorful juice
> *vertu*—virtue, goodness, love, vigor
> *engendred*—strength to bring into being life and its flowering
> *sweete breeth*—sweet, warm, pleasurable breezes

The connotations of Eliot's words reveal a different tone:

> *cruelest*—pain, suffering, distress, anguish
> *breeding*—animal sensuousness, gross copulation
> *dead*—inacitvity, disease, spiritual sterility
> *mixing*—coalescence of remembrance of past inactivity with a desire for it; confused, disordered
> *dull*—sluggish, unfeeling, depressed, tedious

The life forces of April do not "priketh" the poet of *The Waste Land* to life but to memory of, and desire for, the inactivity of winter.

When you read for tone, you will need to read with ear as well as eye. Not only diction but sound is a clue to the author's attitude. The vigorous movement of *The Canterbury Tales* sounds different (indicates a different tone of voice) from the reluctant rhythm of *The Waste Land* (best read, as Eliot himself read it, as if by "an old man in a dry month").

Awareness of the diction and sound of a work may lead you to an awareness of what is perhaps the most significant aspect of tone: *the temperament of the author.* "Fiction," Conrad wrote, "must be . . . the appeal of one temperament to all the other innumerable temperaments whose subtle and resistless power endows passing events with their true meaning. . . ."

An author's words are formulas, correlatives of his individual temperament.

Chaucer, writing in the fourteenth century, exemplifies a temperament in harmony with the movement of nature. Eliot, in the twentieth century (consciously contrasting his vision of April with Chaucer's), ironically expresses emotions divorced, alienated from the movement of nature. Eliot's sophisticated, self-conscious sensibility is evident in what he creates, as is the harmonious sparkle of Chaucer's temperament manifest in his work. A literary work is not only an appeal to temperament but an expression of it.

Meaning and Attitude

Meaning as shown in a speaker's attitude toward his subject can be *explicit* or *ironic*. To distinguish explicit statement from ironic statement is the first step in understanding the speaker's tone.

Explicit Meaning

An author or a character may say directly what he means:

Getting and spending, we lay waste our powers.

This line from William Wordsworth's "The World Is Too Much with Us" intends to mean what it says. In this poem, the poet expresses the idea that the capacity to be emotionally moved by Nature's inherent qualities, the power to see "into the life of things," has been destroyed in us by the energy we expend on the material things of life. We are "out of tune." Nature "moves us not." The statement intends no double meaning. The poet expresses his emotion directly.

Ironic Meaning

Irony, in one form or another, is seldom absent from the great works of literature. Inability to detect irony is, perhaps, one of the most common causes of misreading. Though there is a good deal of overlapping among these terms, four kinds of irony may be distinguished: (1) verbal, (2) situational, (3) cosmic, (4) dramatic.

Verbal Irony An author or a character may speak not explicitly but ironically. That is, the speaker may mean not what he says but the opposite, or something to the oblique, or something complementary to what is stated. **Verbal irony refers to a statement that carries a double meaning.** In *Hamlet* the ghost of Hamlet's father has told Hamlet that his father was poisoned by the king. Hamlet devises a plan to "catch the conscience of the king." He has a group of players present a play which reenacts the actual murder of his father. As the play is being performed, the king becomes disturbed and asks,

Is there no offence in it?

Hamlet replies,

No, no, . . . no offence i' th' world.

The meaning of Hamlet's words is double. He assures the king that there is "no offence," but in addition to this he does not mean that there is "no offence"; he means that there *is* offence. The king, as Hamlet intends, does not catch the second meaning. The statement means two things simultaneously:

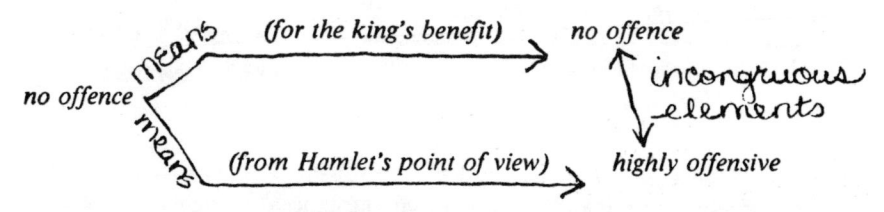

```
                    (for the king's benefit)      no offence
no offence  means ⟨                          ⟩  ↑ incongruous
                    (from Hamlet's point of view) ↓ elements
                                                  highly offensive
```
(annotations: "means" labels on each branch; "incongruous elements" bracketing the two right-hand outcomes)

In Hamlet's deeply tormented emotional state the words suggest still more. His answer refers not only to the murder-play and its intended effect on the king—but also to the effect on Hamlet of the act which has overwhelmed him and to which his imaginative sensibility assigns all events in this world: the murder of his father and marriage of his mother to his uncle, the king. Offensive, yes! And rotten and "rank and gross" and diseased, bestial, monstrous and "remorseless, treacherous, lecherous" may all be implied in the tone of Hamlet's statement. In this case verbal irony serves to express complex and intense emotions.

Situational Irony   Situations as well as statements may be ironic. **Situational irony is a term used to describe a circumstance or a series of events that bring into existence contrasting elements.**

In Ralph Ellison's *Invisible Man* the narrator, who is living in a coal cellar illuminated by exactly 1,369 light bulbs, explains,

> I am invisible ... simply because people refuse to see me.... When they approach me they see only my surroundings, themselves, or figments of their imagination—indeed, everything and anything except me.... That invisibility to which I refer occurs because of a peculiar disposition of the eyes of those with whom I come in contact.... You ache with the need to convince yourself that you do exist....

From his underground residence, the narrator recalls his past: his invisibility as a high school student in the South, as a student in a Negro University, as a laborer in the North, and now as an underground man in a Harlem coal cellar, where he drains off current from Monopolated Light & Power to illuminate his world.

The irony of the narrator's "invisibility" is brought to focus in his situation, in his residence in the coal cellar. Because people have not seen *him*—but only "figments of their imagination"—the narrator has, all his life, been in a hole. But not until he tumbles into the coal cellar—and makes it a warm, well-lighted place by wiring the ceiling with 1,369 lights—does he really see this hole.

> I'm an invisible man and it placed me in a hole—or showed me the hole I was in....

All the narrator's attempts to achieve visibility have "boomeranged" to illuminate his invisibility. But he now sees his invisibility, sees the reality of his blackness in relation to the white world that surrounds him, sees it and affirms it, and to this extent, becomes, for himself, visible. As the lights illuminate the cellar, so the narrator's narrative illuminates his life situation.

the hole makes the narrator invisible
───────────────────────────────── } *incongruous elements*
the hole illuminates the narrator's invisibility and he becomes visible

When reading for situational irony, you will need to recognize elements of contrast and ambiguity that may exist in circumstances or events in a story.

Cosmic Irony An author's primary subject may be not the nature of man or society but the nature of the universe. That is to say, a literary work may make a statement about forces above and beyond man that influence his actions and govern his fate. Toward this subject, as toward all others, an author will reveal an individual tone, a particular attitude. And this tone, or attitude, may be expressed ironically. **Cosmic irony,** then, **refers** not so much to rhetorical statement or dramatic situation (though both are used to convey cosmic irony) but **to the tone of the work as it reveals the author's belief about the nature of things.**

In Thomas Hardy's *Jude the Obscure,* Jude Fawley is caught by the all-encompassing design of the universe. One "fine, warm, and soft summer" afternoon Jude is walking home, dreaming of his future as a classical scholar at Christminster College, "one of those strongholds of learning."

> I will read, as soon as I am settled in Christminster, the books I have not been able to get hold of here: Livy, Tacitus, Herodotus, Aeschylus, Sophocles, Aristophanes . . .

Suddenly, on the other side of a hedge he happens to be passing by, he hears "Ha, ha, ha! Hoity-toity!" and is smacked on the ear with a piece of "soft, cold . . . clammy flesh"—a boar pig's pizzle. Arabella Dunn, a pig-breeder's daughter with "round and prominent bosom and full lips," has been cleaning pig intestines and has thrown the inedible sexual organ (itself ironically symbolic) over the hedge and it has hit Jude. From this point on, Jude's intellectual ambitions are pulverized beneath the "grind of stern reality."

Jude is attracted to Arabella and goes to see her. As they are returning from a walk together one day, Arabella removes from her bosom an egg shell, kept inside a pig bladder in case it should break, and rushes upstairs. Another desire than the one to learn Ancient Greek takes hold of Jude and he rushes after Arabella. The two are married; they are not compatible. Jude attempts suicide, turns to drink, contracts inflammation of the lungs, and one bright, festive, cloudless day dies in his room with the band playing. The antagonistic chance working of the universe, symbolized in the smack on the ear with the pig's pizzle, has brought Jude to this end.

The contrast between Jude's ambition and the working of "things as they are" constitutes the book's cosmic irony.

design of things
───────────── } *incongruous elements*
Jude's ambition

Reading for cosmic irony, you will need to perceive, through the action of the work, the author's belief about the powers that move the universe.

Dramatic Irony **The incongruity in dramatic irony lies in the discrepancy between the knowledge possessed by the audience or reader and that possessed by the character.** The audience knows what is happening, has happened, or will happen; the character does not. The character, in fact, often believes the reverse of the truth. Dramatic irony may include verbal, situational, and cosmic irony—all of which are touched on in the following example from Aeschylus' *Agamemnon*.

Aeschylus could assume his audience's familiarity with the events of the Trojan War. Consequently, his audiences would know—even before the play began—how things turned out for Agamemnon and his family. Agamemnon had killed his daughter as a sacrifice to the gods, had gone off to war, and after ten years of fighting destroyed Troy. And now, swollen with self-importance, he is returning home a conquering hero, to be welcomed by his wife, Clytemnestra. Agamemnon arrives in a chariot with the Trojan princess Cassandra, one of the spoils of war, as his mistress. Clytemnestra rolls out a purple robe for her husband's majestic entry into his palace. Flattered, the proud conqueror enters the palace, where Clytemnestra, motivated by love for her sacrificed daughter and by jealousy of the Trojan mistress, throws a net around him and stabs him to death.

But long before the death cry is sounded on stage from inside the palace, the audience, not Agamemnon, knows his fate. In advance of Agamemnon's return to Greece a herald appears on stage to inform the people that the king is returning home:

> King Agamemnon.
> Give him a good welcome as he deserves,
> Who with the axe of judgment-awarding God
> Has smashed Troy and levelled the Trojan land;
> The altars are destroyed, the seats of the gods,
> And the seed of all the land is perished from it.
> Having cast this halter round the neck of Troy
> The King, the elder son of Atreus, a blessed man,
> Comes . . .

The audience, not the herald, is aware of the double meaning in these words. The audience knows Agamemnon will be given a "welcome" which will bring his death, a "welcome" as Clytemnestra and the "judgment-awarding God" (who has put a curse on the House of Atreus) believe he deserves, the "judgment" to be awarded not by Agamemnon to the Trojans with a "halter" and an "axe," but by his wife to him wtih a net and dagger, a "judgment" which will level him as he has "leveled" the Trojan land.

Herald does not know what awaits Agamemnon } *incongruous elements*
Audience knows

Your ability to read verbal, situational, cosmic, dramatic, and other kinds of irony will depend on your recognition of antithetical elements within a work of literature: the incongruity between statement and fact, assumption and reality, the sublime and the ludicrous, illusion and actuality, belief and truth as these discrepancies are inherent in a word, a speech, a situation, or the total work.

Reading Techniques

Good writers of literature are often subtle, and their subtlety is often hidden in the tone of their voices. To miss the tone is to miss the emotion. And yet to respond to fine tonal qualities requires an ear for the soundless marks of black ink on the white page. In some ways tone is the most elusive aspect of a literary work.

Because sensitivity to tone depends on the impression you receive from diction, syntax, situation, and other elements of a literary work, techniques for discovering and responding to tone are directed to these elements. Outline, diagram, and paraphrase are suggested in the example given below as techniques for clarifying tone.

Describing Diction to Discover Tone

Studying the tone of a work, you will often find it practical to focus your analysis on one word, figure of speech, sentence, or passage to develop evidence for general statements describing the author's attitude toward his subject. In William Faulkner's "A Rose for Emily," Emily Grierson, a slender, erect spinster (whose great-aunt "had gone completely crazy"), takes a sweetheart, Homer Barron, "A big, dark, ready man, with a big voice." "Whenever you heard a lot of laughing ... Homer Barron would be in the center of the group." On Sunday afternoon Miss Emily, "her head high," and Homer, "hat cocked and a cigar in his teeth," drive through town in a horse and buggy. The townspeople muse, "She will marry him. ... She will persuade him yet." When Homer attempts to jilt her, Emily, "her face like a strained flag," quietly poisons him.

Some years later Miss Emily herself dies. The townspeople enter her house, and in a bed in a room "decked and furnished as for a bridal" they find what remains of Homer. The narrator, one of the curious townfolk interested in the affair, comments,

> The body had apparently once lain in the attitude of an embrace, but now the long sleep that outlasts love, that conquers even the grimace of love, had cuckolded him.

The subject of this sentence is most immediately and most concretely Homer's decayed body and Emily's death. The attitude of the speaker toward this subject is revealed, in part, by the figure of speech he has created to describe this conclusion to the "love" affair. Using **metonymy, a figure of speech in which something associated with the subject is used in its place,** the narrator does not name death directly but calls it a "long sleep":

> the long sleep that outlasts love = Death
>
> the long sleep that conquers even the grimace of love = Death

This indirect method of expression separates the speaker from his subject and suggests, perhaps, control and emotional detachment.

The word "cuckolded" endows inanimate death with the very animate action of running off with Emily—and thus, it is implied, leaving Homer the husband of an adultress. This "long sleep" (death), then, is a lover who has stolen Emily from Homer. Homer is dead; unmarried; did not while he was alive want to marry Emily; wanted, in fact, to leave her. And yet the speaker likens the lifeless Homer to a man whose wife has run off with a lover. The attempted jilter, Homer, is jilted.

The distance the narrator sets himself from his subject allows for this bit of sophisticated irony. The tone suggests that these comments may be as much the author's, William Faulkner's, as the narrator's.

A description of tone, it may be noted, necessarily includes references to other aspects of a work, for in one sense everything in a work of literature is tone. One possible description of the tone of Faulkner's sentence follows:

> *Intellectual and emotional complexity.*
>
> *A grotesque irony rendered with high poetic sensibility.*
>
> *A sympathy for the abiding and perverse "dust" of the decayed Southern aristocracy as it is represented through Miss Emily.*
>
> *A splendid and subtle, wry and witty mockery of the results of Homer's brash materialistic ways as they confront the delicate but stubborn decay of the aristocratic southern tradition which Miss Emily represents.*
>
> *A tough-minded objectivity—no sentimental banalities here.*

[handwritten margin note: *in this sentence The speaker's attitude toward his subject reveals*]

Because tone cannot be communicated in other words than those in which it is conveyed, this technique only suggests the complex emotional attitude underlying a passage. Nevertheless, you may find that such a description clarifies your understanding. And because not only the author's temperament but also the reader's temperament is unique, different readers will respond to the same passage in different ways. But it is essential that you know your own personal response.

Writing Suggestions

When writing about the tone of a literary work, you will often find it necessary to base your analysis on such aspects of the work as setting, character, plot, or style. In this way you will find concrete evidence to support the abstract statements you will need to make about the author's temperament or his attitude toward his subject. In preparing a paper on tone, you might ask yourself:

What is suggested about the author's temperament in his selection and description of the setting?—a heavy brooding like the dense steaming African jungle he describes? zestful and piquant like the comparisons he makes—

the Nevada desert likened to a "singed cat" and San Francisco to "heaven on a half shell"? ...
What is the author's attitude toward his central character?—the character experiences the primitive call of the wild, and the author howls in unison with him? the character revels in his oration, and the author sighs? ...
Do the events suggest the author's attitude?—the pure young girl pillows the head of the old prostitute on her virgin breast? in search of Eldorado the character is drawn and quartered? ...
What does the idea of the work say about the author's temperament?—man has the ability to build a heaven here on earth? man's progress is fixed by man's permanent limitations? ...
What is the "resonance" of the work, the feeling that exudes from it?—lilting and gay? somber and gloomy? ...

Interesting papers are often written on the author's use of irony. When writing a paper on irony, be aware of the kind of irony you are dealing with: (1) verbal, (2) situational, (3) cosmic, or (4) dramatic. Know also, and make clear in your writing, the two incongruous elements that compose the irony:

$$\frac{statement}{fact} \rightleftarrows$$

$$\frac{assumption}{reality} \rightleftarrows$$

$$\frac{the\ sublime}{the\ ridiculous} \rightleftarrows$$

$$\frac{illusion}{actuality} \rightleftarrows$$

$$\frac{belief}{truth} \rightleftarrows$$

No matter what facet of tone you are writing about, your paper will probably be stronger if you limit your analysis to one or a few passages and then indicate how this one or these few examples of irony function within the total work.

Imagery

7

IMAGERY appeals to the senses: the *sight* of "walls of shadowy granite, in a gleaming pass"; the *coldness* of a rabbit as he limps "trembling through the frozen grass"; the *taste* of "cups of sack . . . and capons"; the *smell* of "incense bearing trees"; the *sound* of "dewy echoes calling/From cave to cave"; the *movement* of a bird in "his riding/Of the rolling level underneath him steady air and striding/High there"; the *lack of movement* in "We stuck, nor breath nor motion:/As idle as a painted ship/Upon a painted ocean"; the *internal sensation* of "every tongue, through utter drought . . . withered at the root." Your experience of a work of literature will depend to a large extent on your ability to respond to those elements that appeal to the senses.

Types of Imagery

IMAGERY (as used in this chapter) is **a general term that includes literal images and figures of speech.** Both are directed to the senses—but in different ways.

Literal Images

A **literal image** is **a representation in words of a sensory experience.** The representation may imitate or mirror the experience, or it may re-create or reshape the experience. In making a literal image, a writer does with words what a painter does with paint or a sculptor with stone—that is, he produces a likeness, a counterpart, or an interpretation of the presence itself. Thus, the writer presents in words an image of some object or experience. The following passage from Ernest Hemingway's *The Sun Also Rises* contains several literal images:

I took the trout ashore, washed them in the cold, smoothly heavy water above the dam, and then picked some ferns and packed them all in the bag, three trout on a layer of ferns, then another layer of ferns, then three more trout, and then covered them with ferns. They looked nice in the ferns, and now the bag was bulky, and I put it in the shade of the tree.

To create the image of the experience, Hemingway presents a number of concrete details: the primarily *tactile* image of "the cold, smoothly heavy water," the primarily *visual* image of the "three trout on a layer of ferns," and the primarily *kinesthetic* images of taking the trout ashore, packing them in the bag, and putting the bag in the shade of the tree (movement or process may also be considered an image because it appeals to the sensory experience of physical action).

The apparent simplicity of literal images can be deceptive. Each concrete detail of an image must be seen clearly. The Hemingway passage, for example, invites us to respond to the image of the water above the dam: its heaviness, its smoothness, its coldness.

Figures of Speech

Figures of speech (often referred to as figurative imagery) arise from a different process of creation than do literal images. Figurative imagery is not based, as are literal images, on *analysis* (the breaking up of one experience into its parts) but, instead, on *comparison* (the putting together of one experience with another to bring out points of similarity or dissimilarity).[1] *In all comparisons there are two things and a likeness between them. Two things are brought together to form one figurative image.* Included in a comparison, then, are the thing being talked about (A) and the thing it is likened to (B).

Though there are many different kinds of figures of speech, the most common and perhaps the most important are (1) simile, (2) metaphor, (3) personification, (4) overstatement, (5) understatement. An understanding of these five figures of speech provides a basis for understanding all figurative imagery.

Simile Simile is **a figure of speech in which the comparison between two things is directly expressed**—usually by the use of *like* or *as*. Note the simile in the following lines from LeRoi Jones's "Look for You Yesterday, Here You Come Today."

> The sun like a huge cobblestone
> flaking its brown slow rays

"the sun" (A) is likened to "a huge cobblestone" (B)

---

[1] For further discussion see Herbert Read, *English Prose Style* (Boston: Beacon Press, 1955), Chapter 3.

Metaphor   Metaphor is **a figure of speech in which the comparison is not directly expressed but is implied.** Note the following use of metaphor in the first four lines of T.S. Eliot's "The Hollow Men."[2]

>We are the hollow men
>We are the stuffed men
>Leaning together
>Headpiece filled with straw. Alas!

"We" (A) ——are——▸ "hollow men" (B¹)

"We" (A) ——are——▸ "stuffed men" (B²)

Personification   Personification is **a comparison that attributes human characteristics to inanimate objects.** In John Milton's "L'Allegro" the poet addresses Melancholy:

>Hence loathed Melancholy
>   Of Cerberus and blackest midnight born,
>In Stygian cave forlorn
>   'Mongst horrid shapes, and shrieks, and sights unholy,
>Find out some uncouth cell,
>   Where brooding Darkness spreads his jealous wings,
>And the night-raven sings;
>   There upon eban shades, and low-browed rocks,
>As ragged as thy locks,
>   In dark Cimmerion desert ever dwell.

In this passage Melancholy, offspring of the union of Cerberus (a three-headed hound with snakes for hair) and "blackest midnight" in a horrid underworld cave, is told (as if human) to find a suitable place to dwell; "midnight" is capable of giving birth; "Darkness" broods and is jealous; and the "rocks" have foreheads.

Overstatement   Overstatement is **a comparison which uses extravagant exaggeration for a deliberate effect.** In John Donne's "The Canonization" the speaker says,

>Alas, alas, who's injured by my love?
>   What merchant's ships have my sighs drowned?
>Who says my tears have overflowed his ground?
>   When did my colds a forward spring remove?

The speaker, a man in love (who, according to traditional notions of a lover, might be expected to sigh and cry and grow hot and cold), likens

his sighs (A) ——to——▸ *wind storms at sea violent enough to overturn ships* (B)

his tears (A) ——to——▸ *an inundation deep enough to flood someone's land* (B)

his colds (A) ——to——▸ *a freeze sufficient to prevent an early spring* (B)

[2]For a further discussion of this metaphor see Glossary, Tenor and Vehicle.

It is necessary to see clearly what is compared with what in order to respond to the intended effect of these inordinate comparisons.

Understatement   Understatement is **a figure of speech in which a writer creates a deliberate effect by saying less than he actually means.** In the epic poem *Beowulf* there is in Heorot, the great mead-hall of the Danes, feasting, ale drinking, and harp playing. Here brave men live "prosperously in joy"—until the monster Grendel comes out of his fen-home, seizes thirty men, and devours them. For "a long while: twelve winters' space," fear and violence replace mirth and joy at Heorot as Grendel continues to glut himself with the souls of fighting men: "That was great heartbreaking sorrow." But then Beowulf, a man with no small strength in his hands, sails to Denmark to free the land of Grendel. One night Beowulf waits in Heorot. The demon Grendel comes for his periodic feast. Beowulf seizes Grendel by the claw. Grendel tries to pull away. His "shoulder gaped a mighty wound, the sinews sprang assunder—the tendons burst," and Grendel flees to his "fen-fastnesses" to die. At this point the poet says,

> His parting from life did not seem a cause for sorrow.

The poet attains a special emotional impact by using **a negative form of expression.** This is **a special form of understatement** called **litotes.**

did not seem a cause for sorrow   =   *was a joyous occasion*

Because "not . . . sorrow" is used in place of "joy," the poet invites comparison between "sorrow" and "joy" by bringing the two together. The twelve bloody, terror-filled years that preceded Grendel's death emphasize the rejoicing that now follows it—the banquet, the horse racing, the singing, the harp playing, the mead drinking, and the sight of Grendel's shoulder and claw hanging in trophy from the roof of Heorot.

Complex Imagery

Figures of speech are not always as uncomplicated as the above examples of simile, metaphor, personification, overstatement, and understatement may suggest. Your comprehension of some works may depend on your ability to analyze a complex comparison within them.

Imagery may be difficult to understand because the point of comparison between the two things brought together—the subject (A) and the object it is likened to (B)—is not obvious without some probing on the part of the reader. If we let X stand for the point of comparison—that is, for the quality that the subject and the object are meant to have in common; for the quality that gives new meaning to these two elements; or, more simply, for the attributes of (B)—then a figure of speech may be diagrammed this way:

Subject (A) | *Thing subject is likened to (B)*   \\ *Attributes of thing subject is likened to (X)*

In a two-line stanza from T. S. Eliot's dramatic monologue "The Love Song of J. Alfred Prufrock," Prufrock says,

> I should have been a pair of ragged claws
> Scuttling across the floors of silent seas.

Clearly enough, Prufrock (or "I") is compared with "claws." (Here Eliot uses a special kind of metaphor called **synecdoche**, in which **a part stands for the whole**; that is, "claws," an important part of a crab, signifies the whole shellfish). But what are the attributes of the "claws" or of a crab? The metaphor may be diagrammed in two ways:

(1) $\underline{I \mid a\ pair\ of\ ragged\ claws\ /\ Scuttling\ across\ floors}$
    $\underline{of\ silent\ seas\ \setminus\ raw,\ vital,\ instinctive}$

(2) $\underline{I \mid a\ pair\ of\ ragged\ claws\ /\ Scuttling\ across\ floors}$
    $\underline{of\ silent\ seas\ \setminus\ futile,\ submerged,\ old,\ backward}$.

A choice between these two readings depends on how "I should have been" is read. Does Prufrock mean, "I wish I had been like this, although in reality I am not"—that is, "Rather than the timid Prufrock I am, I wish I had been a pair of ragged, scuttling claws—raw, vital, instinctively alive"? Or does Prufrock mean, "I should have been this because by nature I am like this"—that is, "I am weak, old, lifeless; and, instead of a man such as I am, I should have been a helpless, senseless, submerged crab"? That is, does Prufrock believe he is unlike or is like a crab?

Your reading of this complex metaphor will depend on your reading of other passages of the poem, especially on other metaphors ("I am not Prince Hamlet, nor was meant to be;/Am an attendant lord"). There is, perhaps, something in the complex sensibility of Prufrock that causes him to react to his existence in such a way that he ineffectually wishes to be what in reality he sees he is not.

Another reason imagery is often complex is that the parts of a figure of speech may be intricately related. In some imagery there is an almost mathematical relationship of the parts. The elements of such comparisons may be understood in terms of a mathematical proportion such as 2 is to 6 as 3 is to 9 (that is, 2:6 :: 3:9). And thus, a figure of speech may be formulated a:b :: c:d.

One sentence in Joseph Conrad's *Heart of Darkness* indicates where the "meaning" of the story lies. An interpretation based on evidence in the story itself must deal with the intricate use of simile in this one sentence.

> But Marlow was not typical (if his propensity to spin yarns be excepted), and to him the meaning of an episode was not inside like a kernel but outside, enveloping the tale which brought it out only as a glow brings out a haze, in the likeness of one of these misty halos that sometimes are made visible by the spectral illumination of moonshine.

The relationship of the parts of such complex comparisons as this one may be clarified by giving their bare outline in the form of a ratio. Letting the sign : stand for "is related to," the sign $\therefore$ stand for "is not like, or is not similar to," and the sign :: stand for "is like or is similar to," Conrad's comparison may be shown this way:

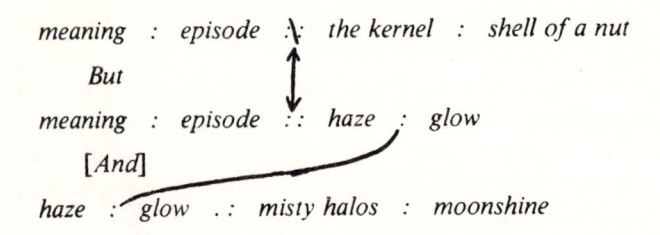

meaning : *episode* $\therefore$ *the kernel* : *shell of a nut*

But

meaning : *episode* :: *haze* : *glow*

[And]

haze : *glow* .: *misty halos* : *moonshine*

Thus, the speaker is saying that in the tale or episode that Marlow is to tell, the meaning is not inside but outside. That is, the meaning is not inside the story as a nut is in its shell. Don't look for the meaning there. But the meaning is outside the tale, enveloping it. Further, the meaning is likened to the haze that envelops a glow. And the tale is likened to the glow that brings out the haze. The meaning and the haze are then further likened to one of those misty halos. The tale and the glow are likened to the moonshine, which makes visible the halos. The meaning of "one of Marlow's inconclusive experiences" is, then, not inside the tale, but outside it, enveloping the tale as a haze envelops a glow, which is like a halo that is illuminated by moonshine.

Few figures of speech are as complex or as rich as the two examples given above. But when they are, diagram and equation may be useful methods for analyzing meaning. It should be noted, however, that an etherized response may be the result of this activity of wrenching a figure of speech from context and laying out its parts. Imagery must not be taken literally; it is poetic, not algebraic. Nevertheless, emotional response rests on knowledge of what exactly is being said about what. By using methods that bring about close analysis, you can often avoid careless or haphazard reading.

Reading Techniques

Provided you use your discretion, you can apply the following techniques to understand imagery more fully. Misuse of the techniques of drawing, listing, and marking may be avoided if two things are kept in mind. First, a technique that is helpful when applied to one image may not be helpful when applied to another. Second, though a figure of speech may be divided into parts for the sake of clarity, every figure of speech is a unit in itself, an "integrity"; and each of these units is, in turn, but a part of the total work in which it appears.

Drawing

Not all imagery is primarily visual, and not all readers will respond visually to most imagery; but in some special cases, sketching imagery clarifies the picture the words on the printed page create in your mind's eye. Figure 10 is a sketch of the following stanza from Matthew Arnold's "Dover Beach":

> The Sea of Faith
> Was once, too, at the full, and round earth's shore
> Lay like the folds of a bright girdle furled.
> But now I only hear
> Its melancholy, long, withdrawing roar,
> Retreating, to the breath
> Of the night-wind down the vast edges drear
> And naked shingles of the world.

The subject of the passage is "The Sea of Faith." The abstract idea of "Faith" may be visualized as a sea. The first three lines of the passage describe the "Sea" as it was in the past. The last five lines (introduced by "But," a word that marks contrasts) describe the "Sea" as it is now in the present. In the past, the "Sea of Faith" was full and "Lay like the folds of a bright girdle furled" (no attempt is made to sketch this simile). In the present, "Faith" can only be heard withdrawing down the pebbled incline of the ocean floor—down the "vast edges drear/ And naked shingles of the world."

No two people will, of course, see or sketch an image in exactly the same way. But sketching an image in the rough may clarify your visualization of it.

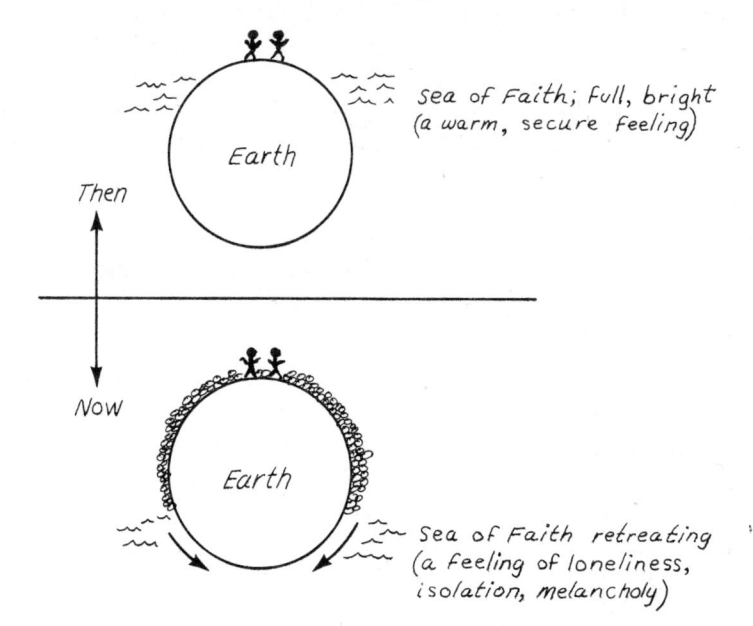

Figure 10 Sketch of Image in "Dover Beach"

Listing

Offering advice to a fellow poet John Keats said, "'load every rift' of your subject with ore." Keats's poetry, like most good poetry, is loaded with literal images. Because of the "fine excess" of literal images in some poetry, the reader must sometimes make special efforts to increase his awareness of them.

Keats's "Ode to a Nightingale" appeals to many different senses. On hearing the nightingale's immortal song, the poet experiences such intense emotion that he longs for a "draught of vintage" so that he might "fade away" with the bird "into the forest dim," away from "The weariness, the fever, and the fret" of this world. Following is the second stanza of the poem. Figure 11 shows one possible listing of its images.

> O, for a draught of vintage! that hath been
>   Cooled a long age in the deep-delvéd earth,
> Tasting of Flora and the country green,
>   Dance, and Provençal song, and sunburnt mirth!
> O for a beaker full of the warm South,
>   Full of the true, the blushful Hippocrene,
>   With beaded bubbles winking at the brim,
>   And purple-stainéd mouth;
> That I might drink, and leave the world unseen,
>   And with thee fade away into the forest dim.

Because one literal image may appeal to more than one of the senses, no rigid classification of images is possible. Sense responses may harmonize, one passing imperceptibly into another. The "draught of vintage," for example, may appeal to a reader's sense of sight, smell, and taste; also, a reader may feel its coolness, may imagine he hears its bubbles breaking, may sense the new internal emotion received from taking in its aged life. The value of listing, then, lies not in classification but in the activity of becoming more aware of your own relation to the images. This awareness will, in turn, have the effect of bringing you to a fuller emotional response to each image as it appears within the context of the whole poem.

Figure 11   Listing of Images
Stanza from "Ode to a Nightingale"

Visual	Auditory	Kinesthetic	Tactile	Smell	Taste
Deep delvéd earth	Provençal song	Bubbles winking	Sunburnt	Flora and country green?	Vintage… tasting of flora?…
Flora and country green	Mirth?	Dance	Warm South		That I might drink
Beaker full beaded bubbles	The blushful Hippocrene / with beaded bubbles?	Cooled a long age?	Cooled?		O for a beaker full?
Purple-stainéd mouth					
Fade away into the forest dim					

You may want to use this technique of listing only when making a special study of a poem, play, short story, or novel in an effort to discover a new key to a reading of the work. You may, for example, discover a **"controlling image"** or an **"image cluster"**; that is, **one image or a number of different images so interfused with the meaning of the work that an awareness of them is central to an understanding of the total work.** In Charles Dickens's *A Tale of Two Cities,* for example, the kinesthetic image of water, wine, and blood "running, running, running" takes on, through repetition throughout the novel, the qualities of a symbol pointing to a dominant theme in the work.

Marking

The essence of a work of literature may lie primarily in its imagery. The more you understand the imagery, the more you will be able to experience the work. Following is an illustration of techniques that may clarify the imagery in John Donne's "A Valediction: Forbidding Mourning." In this poem the poet (so a friend of Donne's has said) is asking his wife not to mourn his parting as he leaves England on a trip to the continent.

> (As) |virtuous men| pass mildly away,
> And whisper to |their souls| to go,
> Whilst some of their sad |friends| do say,
> The breath goes now, and some say, No:
>
> (So) let |us| melt, and make no noise,
> No tear-floods, nor sigh-tempests move,
> 'Twere profanation of our joys
> To tell the |laity| our love.

⎡ As virtuous men whisper to their parting souls, so let you and me do likewise and make no noise when we part.
    (virtuous men : souls :: you : me)
When virtuous men die they die so quietly that their bedside friends do not know they have passed away. In a like manner, when you and I part let the laity not know about our parting or our deep love.
    (virtuous men : friends :: you and I : laity) ⎤

> Moving of th' |earth| brings harms and fears,
> Men reckon what it did and meant;
> (But) trepidation of the |spheres,|
> Though greater far, is innocent.

⎡ movement of the earth = harm and fear (there is implied here a likeness with
            ↑   "sublunary lovers" of the following
            ↓   stanza)
movement of the sphere = innocence (this, it is implied, is like "our" love) ⎤

Dull sublunary lovers' love
    (Whose soul is sense) cannot admit
Absence, because it doth remove
    Those things which elemented it.

But we by a love so much refined
    That our selves know not what it is,
Inter-assured of the mind,
    Care less, eyes, lips, and hands to miss.

$\begin{bmatrix} \text{sublunary lovers' love} \longrightarrow \text{cannot} \longrightarrow \text{admit absence because it depends on the senses} \\ \text{our love} \longrightarrow \text{can} \longrightarrow \text{admit absence because it depends on the mind, not on physical contact} \end{bmatrix}$

Our two souls therefore, which are one,
    Though I must go, endure not yet
A breach, but an expansion,
    Like gold to airy thinness beat.

my soul : your soul | gold to airy thinness beat \ oneness, endurance, preciousness, goldenness, beauty
When we part my soul will be to your soul as is gold when it is beat to airy thinness

If they be two, they are two so
    As stiff twin compasses are two;
Thy soul, the fixed foot, makes no show
    To move, but doth, if th' other do.

And though it in the center sit,
    Yet when the other far doth roam,
It leans and harkens after it,
    And grows erect, as that comes home.

Such wilt thou be to me, who must
    Like th' other foot obliquely run;
Thy firmness makes my circle just,
    And makes me end where I begun.

thy soul | fixed foot of a twin compass \ does not move unless other leg moves
    sits in the center
    leans toward the other leg
    harkens after it
    grows erect when other leg returns
    remains firm

```
my soul | the moving foot of a twin compass \ runs obliquely
                                             \ circles
                                             \ returns to the fixed
                                                              foot
```

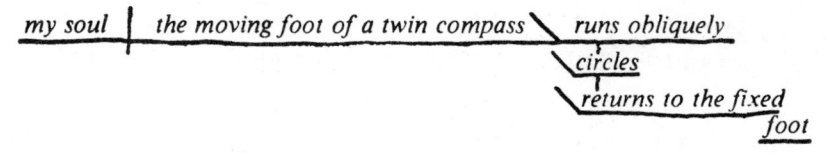

If our souls are not one (like gold to airy thinness beat) but two, then they are like two legs of a divider or a drawing compass. Your soul is the fixed foot and behaves in such and such a way; my soul is the moving foot and behaves in other ways. It is the firmness of your soul that will make my journey perfect—will make it end where it began.

The poem contains four images, each of which advances an argument and expresses the quality of the poet's love for his wife:

(1) soul parting from virtuous man } proposes: do not mourn } all four images reveal the quality of their love
(2) movement of the spheres
(3) gold to airy thinness beat } give reasons for not mourning
(4) twin compasses

Thus, in four unusual comparisons the poet reasons why their parting forbids mourning: with spiritual unity there can be no separation and therefore no reason to mourn. In addition to furthering the argument, each image expresses something more fundamental to the poem, the quality of their love—its spiritual, non-physical essence.

Writing Suggestions

Clues to an understanding of character, style, tone, and symbolism in a work may be rooted in the author's use of imagery. By formulating a statement on the relation of imagery to another aspect of the work, you will have a topic for your paper. Perhaps some of the following questions will furnish some clues.

Is the thing described broken up into its parts, so that each part makes its appeal to the senses?—the evening is green, cool, and warm? the spider is dimpled, fat, and white? ...

What do we see?—"reed-flowers drenched in moonlight"? "imaginary gardens with real toads in them"? ...

What do we hear?—"the sound of a stick upon the floor"? hawks whetting their beaks "clak clak"? ...

What movement do we feel?—"elephants pushing"? "a wild horse taking a roll"? ...

Where in the passage you are analyzing is "like" or "as" used?—the evening is "quiet as a Nun/Breathless with adoration"? the evening is "spread out against the sky/Like a patient etherized upon a table"? ...

Where in the passage you are analyzing is a comparison made without the use of "like" or "as"?—"her eyes were candles burning on a tranquil night"? "her eyes were dry ... deserts"? ...

Is an inanimate object made animate?—Anger is watered with tears, sunned with smiles, and grows? Love "springs/and folds over the world its healing wings"? . . .

Does the passage include extravagant exaggeration?—the speaker says that his hand is so bloody that it will turn the green seas red? he tells us to beget with child a mandrake root? . . .

Is understatement used?—the sword cuts down through the man's helmet, through his breast bone, sinks into the earth, the man falls into two parts; and the poet says, "and that was not a light tap"? "The flute without holes is the most difficult to blow"? . . .

Do the images that a character uses give clues to his mental-emotional state?—you have "not so much brain as ear-wax"? I wish that your "heart be all year like a rose-tree in flower"? . . .

Does one image or do related images recur?—a man is often dressed in clothes too large for him? a little musical phrase is heard at irregular intervals throughout the work? . . .

Your paper will need to be more than a listing of the imagery used in the work you are studying. You will need to formulate an idea which indicates the function of the imagery within the context of the work. This idea will provide focus and give coherence to your discussion.

The body of your paper should support your idea with an analysis of the author's use of literal images (visual, auditory, kinesthetic, tactile, smell, taste, internal sensation) or his use of figures of speech (simile, metaphor, personification, overstatement, understatement).

Rather than attempting to analyze all the imagery in the work, be selective. Perhaps the imagery of smell is outstanding, or the author's use of personification is of special significance. In some cases you may through the analysis of one complex simile discover evidence for the underlying theme of the whole work.

Symbolism

8

A literary **SYMBOL** is **a word or a number of words used to signify a tangible object or event which embodies both concrete and abstract meanings.** The word "rose," for example, when used as a symbol, may refer not only to the flower but to all those things associated with the flower (see Figure 12).

A symbol, then, pulls together two worlds: the visible and the invisible, the material and the immaterial, the concrete and the abstract, the outer world of the senses and the inner world of the imagination. Your job as a reader is to perceive both worlds at once, to see the physical reality and the abstract concept that lies behind it.

Two of the most common errors in reading symbolism are (1) reading into a symbol more than it can reasonably be expected to represent within its context and (2) reading what is not a symbol as if it were a symbol. The first pitfall is clearly illustrated in a dialogue between instructor and student in Lionel Trilling's story "Of This Time, of That Place."

> Blackburn ... looked at his teacher. ... "Do you mean, Doctor Howe, that there aren't two opinions possible?" ...

Figure 12   Symbolic Meanings of "Rose"

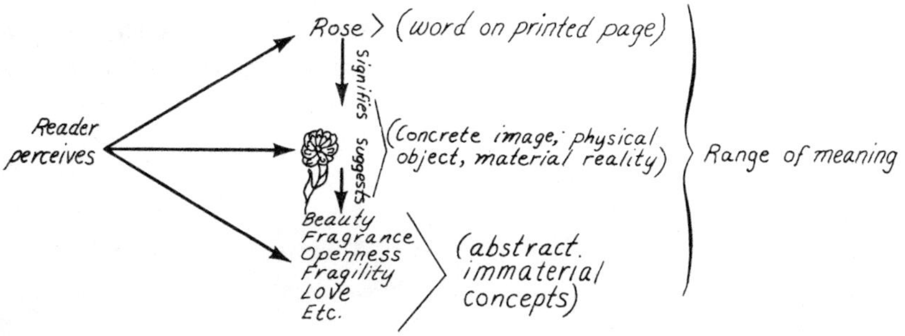

"Yes, many opinions are possible, but not that one. Whatever anyone believes of *The Ancient Mariner,* no one can in reason believe it represents a —a honey-sweet world in which we can relax."

"But that is what I *feel,* sir," . . .

"Look, Mr. Blackburn. Do you really relax with hunger and thirst, the heat and the sea—serpents, the dead men with staring eyes, Life in Death and the skeletons?"

The possible abstract meanings of a symbol are not unlimited but are governed by common sense. Blackburn's wholly subjective readings of the symbolism—serpents, skeletons—is a rewriting of Coleridge's poem, not a reading of it.

The other pitfall, treating what is not a symbol as if it were a symbol, may be illustrated by a passage from Dostoyevsky's *The Possessed*. Kirilov, a member of a fanatic revolutionary group, asks Nickolay Vsyevolodovitch Stavrogin, the main character in the novel,

". . . Have you seen a leaf, a leaf from a tree? . . . I saw a yellow one lately, a little green. It was decayed at the edges. It was blown by the wind. When I was ten years old I used to shut my eyes in the winter on purpose and fancy a green leaf, bright with veins on it, and the sun shining. . . ."

"What's that? An allegory?"

"N-no . . . I'm not speaking of an allegory, but of a leaf, only a leaf. . . ."

When an author names an object—a leaf, for example—most of the time he means, as Kirilov meant, just that, a leaf. And if he means more than a leaf, he also means a leaf, just a leaf; for symbolism is a bringing together of the abstract and the concrete, and the concrete should not be overlooked. In literature abstract statements sometimes stand by themselves; but when they do, they are not symbols. The two pitfalls of reading too much into a symbol and of mistaking what is not a symbol for a symbol can be avoided by careful attention to context.

Emphasis and Symbolism

An author may use an object or a word in his story not so much as a symbol but as a device to emphasize meaning. An object which emphasizes meaning does not exactly stand for or embody an abstract idea as much as it gives weight to and stresses an idea or feeling prominent in the work. **An object used as emphasis reinforces and stresses meaning; an object used as a symbol stands for and embodies meaning.** The distinction between the two is relative. Emphasis is meaning on its way to becoming symbolism.

In the poem "The Fiend" by James Dickey, a leaf of a tree means something more than just a leaf; yet it does not mean quite enough to take on the stature of a symbol. The fiend, "moodily walking head down/ A worried accountant," takes on fresh life as he swarms up a tree to peep through leaves into apartment windows to watch a "shopgirl get ready to take a shower."

In that moon he stands . . . covered with leaf-shapes

The leaves of the tree emphasize the perverse excitement of the fiend as he rises—almost mythically, ritually beneath the moon—in response to the scenes he peers in on.

> But at last he will shed his leaves

The leaves emphasize his invisible life as an excited voyeur, a life which he now abandons to commit forcefully the violent visions he imaginatively acted in the leaves.

In Ernest Hemingway's *A Farewell to Arms,* leaves not only emphasize, as they do in Dickey's poem, but stand for, and thus symbolize, one of the meanings of the novel. The action of the story centers on the love affair of Lieutenant Frederick Henry and Catherine Barkley, a love affair that ends with death and loneliness. The first paragraph of the novel includes the following sentences:

> Troops went by the house and down the road and the dust they raised powdered the leaves of the trees. The trunks of the trees too were dusty and the leaves fell early that year and we saw the troops marching along the road and the dust rising and leaves, stirred by the breeze, falling and the soldiers marching and afterward the road bare and white except for the leaves.

Here at the beginning of the novel, the leaves, choked by the dust raised by marching troops and caught by the forces of autumn, fall to remain alone on the bare, white road. At the end of the novel, Lieutenant Henry—who has been wounded in the war, nursed by Catherine, and who, with Catherine, has fled the war—sees Catherine hemorrhage to death following the stillbirth of their child and walks alone "back to the hotel in the rain." Lieutenant Henry's response to both the leaves and Catherine's death is a painful but stoical understanding of life. Both the love affair and the leaves are buffeted by the chaos of war and killed by the tragic conditions of life. The leaves symbolize the love affair and the nature of life itself.

In E. M. Forster's *Howards End* a tree and its leaves are more completely symbolic than are the leaves in *A Farewell to Arms.*

> ... the wych-elm ... was neither warrior, nor lover, nor god. ... It was a comrade, bending over the house, strength and adventure in its roots, but in its utmost fingers tenderness, and the girth, that a dozen men could not have spanned, became in the end evanescent, till pale bud clusters seemed to float in the air.

The wych-elm stands for "the genius" of the farmhouse, Howards End, which maintains the tradition of old England—in contrast to the new England of "electric lights," which "sizzled and jagged in the main thoroughfares" of London. The leaves of the tree represent "tenderness" and are related to the spirit of old Mrs. Wilcox, who while alive "had kept proportion," had given the "idea of greatness," had lived the life of the spirit—in contrast to the modern men, who had "lost the life of the body and failed to reach the life of the spirit," those "hurrying men who know so much and connect so little," who were "excitable without love" and in whose hearts there was "continued flux." The tree embodies the abstract qualities of solidity, proportion, tenderness, and love. And its leaves, "its utmost fingers," "transcend" and "dwarf" the flux of the new England. The wych-elm is a complete symbol. The outward world of the author's sense perceptions and the inward world of his imagination are embodied in the tree. The feelings and ideas which Forster would be unable to state in many pages of generalizations he symbolized in a few words by allowing a concrete object, the wych-elm, to stand for them.

In *The Possessed* Kirilov's leaf is neither emphasis nor symbol. In "The Fiend" the leaves that hide Dickey's peeping tom are used mainly as emphasis. In *A Farewell to Arms* the fallen leaves may be considered emphasis become symbolism. And in *Howards End* the wych-elm is a full-blown symbol. Though the difference between emphasis and symbol is one of degree, it is useful to be aware of the distinction; for few objects in a work of literature are complete symbols, but many emphasize meaning.

Discovering and Interpreting Symbols

A symbol may appear in a work of literature in a number of different ways to suggest a number of different things. Most commonly a symbol will present itself in the form of (1) a word, (2) a figure of speech, (3) an event, (4) the total action. And the symbol may suggest or represent a *situation,* and *idea,* an *emotion.* Your task as a reader will be to find the symbols and to understand their function within the context of the work.

A Word as a Symbol

When using a single word as a symbol an author will often emphasize the word by repeating it. Following is an example of the use of repetition to call attention to a word which signifies an object which, in turn, embodies both concrete and abstract meanings. From the opening paragraphs of Charles Dickens's *Bleak House:*

> Fog everywhere. Fog up the river, where it flows among green aits and meadows; fog down the river, where it rolls defiled among the tiers of shipping, and the waterside pollutions of a great (and dirty) city. Fog on the Essex marshes, fog on the Kentish heights. Fog creeping into the cabooses of collier-brigs; fog lying out on the yards, and hovering in the rigging of great ships; fog drooping on the gunwales of barges and small boats. Fog in the eyes and throats of ancient Greenwich pensioners, wheezing by the firesides of their wards; fog in the stem and bowl of the afternoon pipe of the wrathful skipper, down in his close cabin; fog cruelly pinching the toes and fingers of his shivering little 'prentice boy on deck. Chance people on the bridges peeping over the parapets into a nether sky of fog, with fog all round them. . . .
>
> The raw afternoon is rawest, and the dense fog is densest, and the muddy streets are muddiest, near that leaden-headed old obstruction, appropriate ornament for the threshold of a leaden-headed old corporation: Temple

Bar. And hard by Temple Bar, in Lincoln's Inn Hall, at the very heart of the fog, sits the Lord High Chancellor in his High Court of Chancery.

Never can there come fog too thick, never can there come mud and mire too deep, to assort with the groping and floundering condition which this High Court of Chancery, most pestilent of hoary sinners, holds, this day, in the sight of heaven and earth.

On such an afternoon, if ever, the Lord High Chancellor ought to be sitting here—as here he is—with a foggy glory round his head....

In the High Court the litigation of the suit of *Jarndyce and Jarndyce* has been muddling on for generations—pinching, suffocating, destroying the lives of numerous people dependent upon the outcome of the suit. In this High Court sits the Lord High Chancellor, "mistily engaged in one of ten thousand stages of an endless cause ... groping knee-deep in technicalities ... with bills, cross-bills, answers, rejoinders, injunctions, affidavits, issues, references ... reports, mountains of costly nonsense." This is the *situation*, the conditions under which the story opens. The fog—enveloping, stifling, smothering everything—is a cognate for this *situation*.

In addition to emphasizing the situation, the fog suggests the predominant *emotion* of the novel: worn-out, exhausted, overthrown, the hopes of the litigants sink in a mass of legal fog. And still more, the fog may be seen to symbolize the *idea* of the novel: present life is strangled by the dead hand of the past. The novel presents a world in which "patience, courage, [and] hope" are unable to breathe, a world in which brain and heart are overturned and smothered, a world in which the obsolete past fogs in the present. The one word *fog,* then, symbolizes a situation, an emotion, and an idea. The word refers not only to a large mass of condensed water vapor but to much more. (See Figure 13.)

Figure 13 Symbolic Meanings of "Fog"

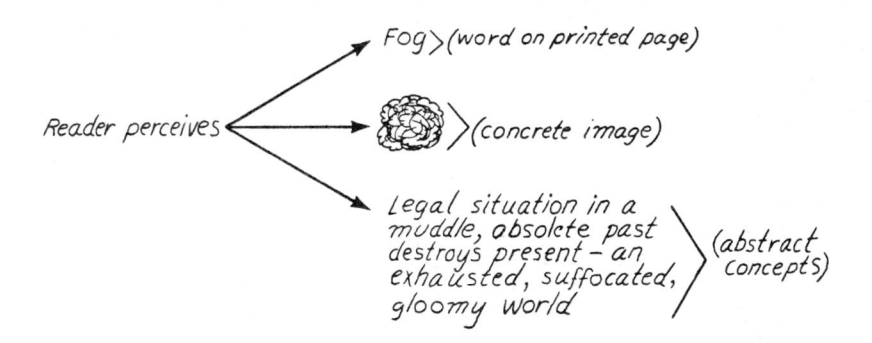

Reader perceives →
- Fog > (word on printed page)
- (concrete image)
- Legal situation in a muddle, obsolete past destroys present — an exhausted, suffocated, gloomy world > (abstract concepts)

A Figure of Speech as a Symbol

In a figure of speech one thing is likened to another thing, and by way of this likeness an abstract *idea* is suggested. When the abstract idea is a dominant theme in the literary work, the figure of speech may take on the significance of a symbol.

In Goethe's *Faust,* the Devil (Mephistopheles), affecting politeness and sentiment, chats with God about man:

> He seems to me—if your Honour does not mind—
> Like a grasshopper—the long-legged kind—
> That's always in flight and leaps as it flies along
> And then in the grass strikes up its same old song.
> I could only wish he confined himself to the grass!
> He thrusts his nose into every filth, alas.

Here in the opening lines of this poetic drama, man is likened to a grasshopper. Though the comparison is not repeated again in the drama, its significance becomes apparent as action, character, and thought develop the theme that "Men make mistakes as long as they strive"; but it is by way of this imperfect, wayward groping (so distateful to the devil) that man finds salvation. Man's flights and leaps are evidence of "the little soul, Psyche with wings." But the wings, the incessant, imperfect, aspiring essence of man, are of the "primal source"; and Mephistopheles, frustrated by Faust's "moving on", by his discontented activity, complains,

> By no joy sated, filled by no success,
> Still whoring after shapes that flutter past.

The comparison, then, of man as a flying, leaping insect is symbolic, as is the total drama, of the fundamental nature of the human spirit—of its struggling, aspiring, storming essence. (See Figure 14.)

Because a figure of speech has the power to condense thought and communicate emotion, an author will often use it as a device for revealing both meaning and feeling. Your analysis of a figure of speech within its context may provide a sound basis for the interpretation of the symbolic meaning of a whole work.

An Event as a Symbol

A single action a character performs may suggest an abstract meaning beyond the physical act itself. Not only a word or a figure of speech but an event, a particular happening, may be symbolic.

Figure 14   Symbolic Meanings of "Grasshopper" Simile

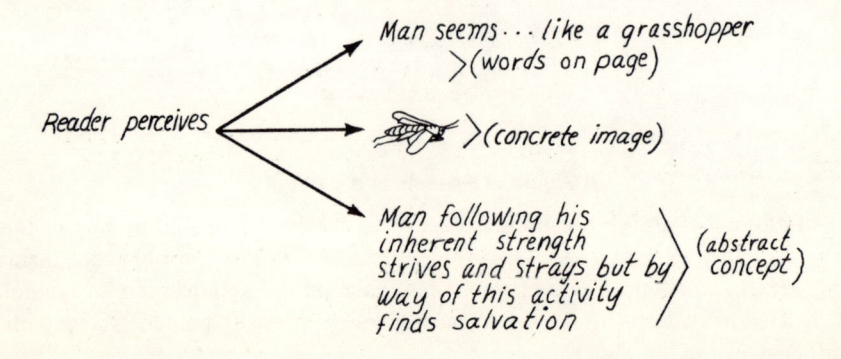

Reader perceives:
- Man seems... like a grasshopper (words on page)
- 🦗 (concrete image)
- Man following his inherent strength strives and strays but by way of this activity finds salvation (abstract concept)

Peer Gynt, the protagonist of Henrik Ibsen's drama *Peer Gynt,* is a swaggering, boastful Norwegian farmboy, an adventurous, lovable rascal who "when the work is at busiest" goes off "to prowl about the hills." In quest of self-fulfillment Peer undertakes one adventure after another: he steals another man's bride, "carrying her under his arm like a pig" to scramble up a mountain "for his rape"; deserts her; marries another; deserts her; lives with a girl, Solveig, in a hut in the forest; leaves her to venture forth—to sell slaves in America and idols in China, to be deserted in Africa by a dancing girl who has "extravagances that tickle a palate that's sated with what is normal"; and finally, after years of exciting experiences, returns to Norway to find the aged Solveig waiting for him.

Alone one day in front of Solveig's hut Peer, on "all-fours . . . grubbing up wild onions," says to himself:

Peer . . . you're an onion! Now my dear Peer, I'm going to peel you . . . *(Takes an onion and peels it, layer by layer)*

With each layer Peer names an adventure in his life.

(Pulls off several more layers together) There's a most surprising lot of layers! Are we never coming to the kernel?

(Pulls all that is left to pieces.) There isn't one! To the innermost bit it's nothing but layers smaller and smaller. Nature's a joker!

Not the odor or the taste but the form of the onion, as Peer discovers as he peels it, represents his life and being: layer upon layer of adventure with no core. Peer has selfishly lived the motto "To thyself be enough." But "Self is only found" as Solveig has found it, "by being lost, gained by being given away." The onion-peeling incident symbolizes Peer's adventurous life and the result of it. (See Figure 15.)

The Total Action as a Symbol

Sometimes not only a word, a figure of speech, or an event but the total action of a work is symbolic. In Franz Kafka's "The Hunger Artist," the "artist" is

Figure 15 Symbolic Meaning of "Onion-Peeling Incident"

Reader perceives →
- ... you're an onion ... etc. (words on printed page or spoken words and action on stage)
- (concrete image or action on stage)
- Peer is hollow at the core. He has no self. (abstract concept)

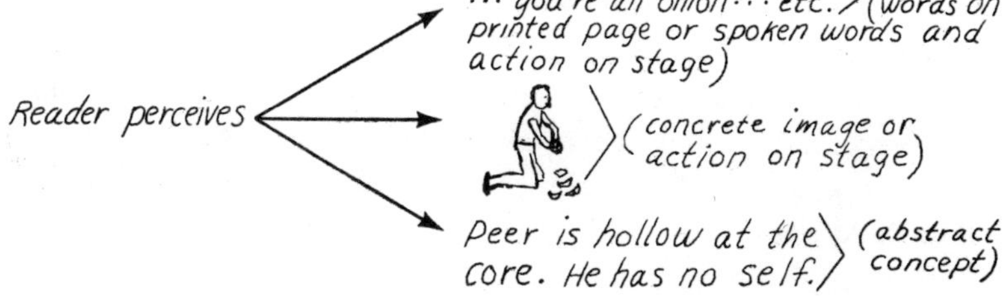

devoted to the activity of fasting, his profession and his sole occupation in life. "Pallid in black tights, with his ribs sticking out," he sits on a pile of straw in a small cage, fasting. On the fortieth day of his fast, with a band playing, he is helped out of his cage by two young ladies. He shakes, totters, and sways, his "little bunch of knucklebones" supported by the trembling hand of one of the "blenching" ladies. A little food is put between the artist's lips and the fast is over. But the artist is dissatisfied. He is "troubled in spirit," not because of the pain of the fast but because he wishes to fast longer. His manager, however, has fixed the length of each fast at forty days, for it has been found that after this time the public loses all interest. Some decades later, when interest in fasting has declined, the hunger artist, deserted by his public, hires himself out to a circus where he may fast as long as he likes. But at the circus the spectators throng past the artist's cage to the menagerie where the animals roar "at feeding times," devouring "raw lumps of flesh." The hunger artist fights "against this lack of understanding, against a whole world of non-understanding." He "fasts on and on," not counting the days—until one day an attendant remembers him and, poking through the straw with a stick, finds him:

> "Are you still fasting?" . . . "Forgive me everybody," whispered the hunger artist. . . . "I have to fast . . . I can't help it . . . I couldn't find the food I liked. If I had found it, believe me, I should have made no fuss and stuffed myself like you or anyone else."

The artist is buried, "straw and all," and a panther, "the joy of life" in his jaws, is given the cage.

Fasting is the hunger artist's personal response to the conditions of life, to the world as he feels it. Only through fasting can the artist express himself; and thus it is only through this activity that he can be understood. The artist would not fast if he could avoid it, but there is no food he wants; he would do as others do, but he cannot. This conflict in the artist's emotions is shown in his art, in his fast. And it is this that he asks to be forgiven for. He feels guilty because he does not hunger for the common food that others find joy in; and yet he hungers for others' understanding of his lack of desire for that common food. The fast is, then, a cry for understanding, for acknowledgement, for love. It is a symbol of the artist's inner emotional world—caged, isolated, alone, craving understanding, fasting for it, feeling guilty in his need for it, and, in the end, completely without it. The whole story is a symbol for this complex and ambivalent emotion. (See Figure 16.)

To sum up, the one *word* "fog" in Dickens's *Bleak House* symbolizes the situation, emotion, and idea of the novel; the *figure of speech*, man "seems . . . like a grasshopper," symbolizes the main idea of Goethe's *Faust;* the *event* or the action of Peer Gynt's peeling the onion symbolizes the idea of Ibsen's drama; and the *total action* of "The Hunger Artist," his fasting, symbolizes the emotion of Kafka's story.

Figure 16   Symbolism in "The Hunger Artist"

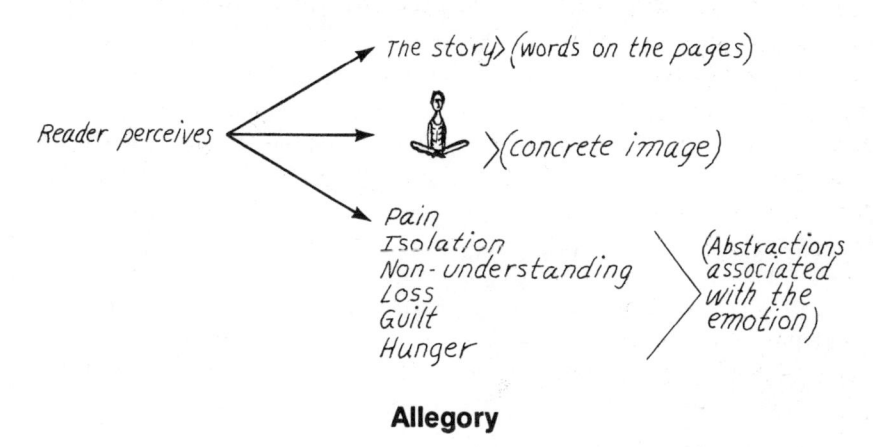

Reader perceives →
- The story (words on the pages)
- (concrete image)
- Pain, Isolation, Non-understanding, Loss, Guilt, Hunger (Abstractions associated with the emotion)

Allegory

Allegory is a kind of literary work closely related to symbolism. **Allegory is a narrative that communicates abstract concepts** (usually, moral ideas) **by presenting them in concrete terms.** In Plato's *Republic*, Socrates says, "Let me show in a figure how far our nature is enlightened or unenlightened." To set forth the concept of enlightenment Socrates tells a story in which he uses such concrete details as a cave, men, chains, shadows, and the sun. Men chained in an underground cave watch shadows reflected on the wall of the cave. One of the men is liberated from his chains and makes a slow ascent out of the cave. At first the light of the outside world hurts his eyes. But eventually his eyes become accustomed to the light, and he is able to look at the Sun itself—the Sun "that produces the seasons and the course of the year and controls everything," and provides the knowledge necessary to act with wisdom in this life. The man, it is then imagined, returns to his former place in the cave. But, because his eyes are still filled with the light of the sun, he is unable to compete successfully with the other prisoners in their game of giving their opinions of the shadows reflected on the wall of the cave.

After he has finished his tale, Socrates says that the cave "is the world of sight," and it represents the prison house of the unenlightened. The sun is the "idea of the good," and it represents the "intellectual world" of the enlightened. To become enlightened we who are living in this prison house of the senses have the possibility of turning around and making our journey upward toward enlightenment. Socrates' allegory is, then, a coded version of a philosophical idea.

Like symbolism, allegory is a fusion of the abstract and the concrete. However, with allegory the author does not begin with a rendering of the real world, in which he finds objects to suggest his abstract meanings; instead, he begins with an abstract concept, which he expounds in concrete terms in a narrative. The allegorist begins with the abstract; the symbolist, with the concrete (this distinction, it should be remembered, is one of degree). Socrates begins with the inanimate, abstract idea of enlightenment and by the use of allegory communicates that idea through the animate, concrete terms of narrative, setting, and character.

Another way to look at allegory is as expanded metaphor. ("By metaphors I speak," John Bunyan said.) Or more specifically, allegory is expanded personification. Character, action, and setting in an allegory may be viewed as personified abstractions or, to put it another way, as animated ideas. In Bunyan's *The Pilgrim's Progress* Christian (the aspiring Christian soul, the "Plain Man") carrying a bundle of sins on his back undertakes a journey (the Christian life, the "Pathway to Heaven") that carries him through a number of different places (states of the struggling soul, inner moral obstacles). On one part of his journey Christian and his traveling companion, Pliable, fall into a bog, the Slough of Despond:

> ... and Christian, because of the burden that was on his back, began to sink in the mire. ...
> At that Pliable began to be offended, and angrily said to his fellow, Is this the happiness you have told me all this while of? [Pliable struggles out of the bog and quits the journey.]
> Wherefore Christian was left to tumble in the Slough of Despond alone: but ... a man came to him, whose name was Help, and asked him what he did there? ... Help gave him his hand, and drew him out, and set him upon sound ground, and bid him go on his way.

The moral attitudes of pliancy and help, endowed with the attributes of feeling and action, have become human beings. And the despondent emotional state of the aspiring soul has been personified as a murky bog in which man may fall on his perilous journey from the City of Destruction to the Celestial City. With the primary purpose of communicating abstract concepts, Plato and Bunyan created situations, characters, and concrete objects.

Reading Techniques

If it is a mistake to fly to abstract, symbolic meanings without first clearly seeing the specific, concrete details, it is also a mistake to become so engrossed in concrete details that abstract implications go unperceived. A literary work of quality, however, embodies both concrete and abstract meanings; and if we are to read with understanding and enjoyment, it is necessary to be aware of the many meanings inherent in a work.

By listing concrete details which embody the abstract meaning of a work, you may—through an awareness of the many different concretions that embody one abstraction—bring yourself to a fuller, more comprehensive reading of that work.

Diagramming and Listing Concrete
Details Embodying the Abstract Idea of a Work

An author may use many symbols to emphasize one central idea. In Frank Norris's *McTeague,* for example, both large symbols and subordinate symbols appear. Obvious and not quite so obvious symbols occur on almost every page of the novel.

Symbolism   89

The main character, McTeague, works as a car boy in a mine with his father, who every other weekend becomes "a beast, a brute, crazy with alcohol." Because a charlatan dentist happens through the mining camp and fires "Mrs McTeague's ambition ... for her son to rise in life and enter a profession," the dull, slow-witted McTeague learns to pull teeth, moves to San Francisco, and sets up a dental practice.

By chance, Trina Sieppa's front tooth is broken. Because her cousin Marcus Schouler happens to know McTeague, Trina goes to McTeague's Dental Parlors to have the roots of the broken tooth extracted. Goverened by instinct, McTeague falls in love with Trina; ruled by emotions, Trina surrenders to him. The two are engaged, Trina wins a five-thousand-dollar lottery ticket, and they are married.

An underlying greed comes to the surface to control Trina; an underlying brute violence bursts forth to control McTeague. One night, crazy with alcohol, McTeague murders Trina and takes her lottery winnings. Fleeing the law, McTeague blindly follows a cow trail and ends up in the heart of blazing Death Valley. There he is found by Schouler, who, seized by hatred and jealousy for McTeague, has tracked him down. In a struggle for the sack containing Trina's five thousand dollars, Schouler dies beneath blows from McTeague's fists; but as he does, he handcuffs McTeague's wrist to his own. Exhausted, without water, and handcuffed to a dead body, McTeague stands "stupidly looking around" while all about him "stretch the measureless leagues of Death Valley."

This, in brief, is the action of the novel, and it illustrates the central idea. But even more than the action, the generous use of symbols and subsymbols animates and communicates the idea given in the following key passage from the novel:

> From the first McTeague and Trina had not sought each other. Chance had brought them face to face, and mysterious instincts as ungovernable as the winds of heaven were at work knitting their lives together. Neither of them had asked that this thing should be, that their destinies, their very souls, should be the sport of chance. If they could have known, they would have shunned the fearful risk. But they were allowed no choice in the matter.

This abstract idea may not be fully comprehended unless it is perceived through the symbols; and, in reverse, the symbols may not be apparent as symbols unless read with the abstract idea in mind. A vertical movement of the reader's mind is called for, an up-and-down movement between abstract and concrete. When many symbols are present in a work, as they are in *McTeague* (in this novel Norris uses such disparate things as hands, a billiard ball, a song), it is sometimes helpful to diagram their relationship to the abstract idea, as in Figure 17.

Once you have seen the relationship between the abstract idea and the symbols, you may wish to focus on a few of the symbols and to clarify them by outlining them in a way similar to the one given below:

> *Opening description of McTeague*
> His hands were enormous, red, and covered with a fell of stiff, yellow hair; they were hard as wooden mallets, strong as vises, the hands of the old-time car boy. ... His head was square-cut, angular; the jaw salient, like that of the carnivora.

Chapter Eight

Symbols or subsymbols	Relation to abstract idea
enormous hands *salient jaw* ⟶	Heredity and environment control McTeague. "Below the fine fabric of all that was good in him ran the foul stream of hereditary evil, like a sewer. The vices and sins of the father.... The evil of an entire race." "The brute within."

Courting Trina, McTeague visits the Sieppe house

> In the backyard was a contrivance for pumping water from the cistern.... It was a dog wheel, a huge, revolving box in which the unhappy black greyhound spent most of his waking hours.... Mrs. Sieppe threw lumps of coal at him, waking him to his work.

greyhound ⟶ man driven by forces outside himself

Trina and McTeague walking by the railroad tracks

> Suddenly he took her in his enormous arms.... Then Trina gave up all in an instant.... A roar and a jarring of the earth suddenly grew near and passed them in a reek of steam and hot air. It was the Overland with its flowing headlight on its way across the continent.

Overland train ⟶ instinct controls

Trina leaves McTeague and rushes home to

> burst in upon her mother... setting a mousetrap in the kitchen.... Mrs. Sieppe set down the mousetrap with such violence that it sprung with a sharp snap.

mousetrap ⟶ Trina is caught, as is mankind, by inner defects over which there is no control.

McTeague, drunk, his "enormous fists, clenched"

> Trina lay unconscious, just as she had fallen under the last of McTeague's blows, her body twitching with an occasional hiccup that stirred the pool of blood in which she lay face downward. Toward morning she died with a rapid series of hiccups that sounded like a piece of clockwork running down.

clockwork ⟶ Trina moves, as does everyone, only as she can in accordance with the make-up of her parts—until the movement stops.

Story ends with canary in cage which McTeague has carried with him throughout the novel

> McTeague remained stupidly looking around him, now at the distant horizon, now at the ground, now at the half-dead canary chittering feebly in its little gilt prison.

canary in a cage ⟶ All the characters, all mankind is like this canary in its gilt prison.

McTeague's hands, his salient jaw, the greyhound on a wheel, the roaring train, the mousetrap, the "clockwork running down," the canary in his cage are all symbols, or subsymbols, which suggest the abstract idea of the novel—that man is governed by instinct and chance, that he is a machine without freedom of the will. The symbols are the idea.

Symbolism   91

Figure 17. Symbolism: Concrete Details for Abstract Ideas McTeague

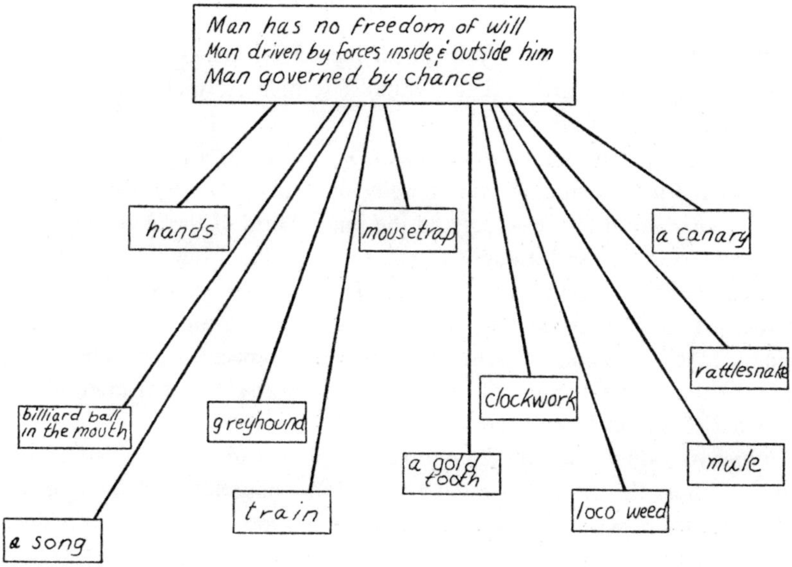

```
                Man has no freedom of will
                Man driven by forces inside & outside him
                Man governed by chance

    hands          mousetrap              a canary

                                               rattlesnake
  billiard ball
  in the mouth   greyhound      clockwork
                              a gold              mule
                              tooth
                                        loco weed
  a song         train
```

Writing Suggestions

The first step in writing a paper on symbolism is to find the symbols. The following questions may help you locate the symbols in the work you are reading.

Does an object suggest an idea?—an iceberg symbolizes a blind force, an "Immanent Will" governing the universe? a green wing represents the concept that an author's creation grows out of his pain and suffering? . . .

Does an object carry with it certain emotions?—a peg-leg suggests the defiant monomania of its owner? a gold hat emphasizes the wearer's desire to please a woman? . . .

Does a situation represent an idea?—people standing along the shoreline looking out to sea represent the watch mankind keeps on the truth it cannot see? . . .

Is a setting used as emphasis?—"the lone and level sands" stretch far away to suggest man's vanity? "beds of roses and a thousand fragrant posies" emphasize the happiness the lovers can attain? . . .

Is a character's inner world represented by the objects that surround him?—the furniture in the man's home is big, heavy, and thick? the glass collection of a crippled girl is exquisitely fragile? . . .

Does the work symbolize its author's inner world?—the carcasses, the city garbage, the muddy road he writes of symbolize his efforts to make poetry of the agonies of his spirit? a man, fasting for love and understanding, symbolizes the author's anxieties and frustrations? . . .

Is one small action in a work symbolic?—a rat is chased, cornered, and killed with a frying pan? a fading star receives a prayer from a dead man's hand?

Is the total action of a work symbolic?—the knight ventures forth, encounters test after test of his honor, and lays his head on the chopping block in fulfillment of his pledge? a man is swallowed by a whale, journeys along the bottom of the slimy ocean, and is spit up on dry land? . . .

Before beginning to write your paper, be certain that what you have selected to analyze as symbols are actually symbols. Remember that not everything in a work of literature is a symbol.

A symbol may appear in a work as (1) a word, (2) a figure of speech, (3) an event, (4) the total action. It will embody both concrete and abstract meanings, both the outer world of the senses and the inner world of the imagination. To confirm for yourself that something is a symbol, formulate a statement of the abstract idea or describe the emotion it embodies. This will also enable you to make clear for yourself to what degree the object or events you are describing emphasize meaning or serve as complete symbols. You will also need to remember to read the symbol within context. Symbols are not open to any personal interpretation the reader may desire to give them.

Limit your discussion to the symbolic meaning of one or a few words or events. Determine how the symbol is related to action, character, and thought. A statement about the function of the symbol within the total work may provide a topic and serve to coordinate and govern the organization of your paper.

Structure

9

In one sense the term **STRUCTURE** refers to **the arrangement of the larger parts of a literary work.** In another sense (because the arrangement of parts arises out of the interrelationship of the various elements) the term **STRUCTURE** refers to **the total work, to the complex interaction of all the various materials that shape a work of literature.** Though it is useful to keep both meanings of the term in mind, it will be practical for our purposes here to emphasize the first, more specific definition of structure as the organization of the major parts of a work.

By stressing the organization of parts, the following marking of George Herbert's "Virtue" may help clarify the idea of structure.

"This is the way things are with the whole world"

> Sweet day, so cool, so calm, so bright
>   The bridal of the earth and sky;   *lives*
> The dew shall weep thy fall tonight; *dies*
>   For thou must die.
>
> Sweet rose, whose hue, angry and brave,
>   Bids the rash gazer wipe his eye: *lives*
> Thy root is ever in the grave,   *dies*
>   And thou must die.
>
> Sweet spring, full of sweet days and roses,
>   A box where sweets compacted lie;   *lives*
> My music shows ye have your closes,   *dies*
>   And all must die.

"But this is the way things are with the virtuous soul"

> Only a sweet and virtuous soul,
>   Like seasoned timber, never gives;
> But though the whole world turn to coal,   *lives*
>   Then chiefly lives.

93

The poem is composed of four stanzas of four lines each. The first two lines of stanzas I, II, and III are concerned with life, the last two lines with death. The first three stanzas are parallel in the sense that each begins with "sweet" and ends with "die." The climactic fourth stanza, however, is not parallel but in opposition to the first three stanzas. Stanza four begins not with "Sweet" but "Only," and ends not with "die" but "lives." The subject of the last stanza (a "virtuous soul") is set off against the subjects of the first stanzas (a "day," a "rose," a "spring").

The organization of the major parts of the poem brings together and holds in suspension, like a taut bow, that which dies (the day, the rose, the spring) with that which lives (the soul). The physical and the spiritual are contrasted. The poem's emotion and thought could not be communicated in another verbal structure than the one in which it is. To change the structure of the poem would be to alter its effect. Thus, the unique quality of the total poem is expressed economically, symmetrically, pictorially through the arrangement and interrelationship of its parts.

Kinds of Structure

All elements of a work of literature function to determine its structure. One element, however, more than any other may stand out to reveal the way parts have been selected and arranged. Following are examples of what are predominantly (1) thematic, (2) logical, (3) emotional structure.

Thematic Structure

An abstract idea may be the dominant force determining the selection, arrangement, and coherence of various elements of a work. A study of structure, then, may involve an analysis of an idea as it manifests itself in a literary work.

In his preface to *Arms and the Man* George Bernard Shaw states the theme of the play: "the realistic morality of the play provides a ... general onslaught on idealism ... which is only a flattering name for romance in politics and morals. ... To me the tragedy and comedy of life lie in the consequences ... of our persistent attempts to found our institutions on the ideals suggested to our imaginations." The structure of *Arms and the Man* is shaped by Shaw's presentation of this idea.

In Act I of this three-act play, the theme of romantic and anti-romantic attitudes toward war and love is introduced. In a "lady's bedchamber in Bulgaria," Raina, the heroine of the play, receives news from her mother of "A great battle ... A victory! and it was won by Sergius," who gloriously led the Bulgarians in a cavalry charge "with their swords and eyes flashing, thundering down like an avalanche" to scatter "the wretched Serbs."

> It proves that all our ideas were real after all. ... Our ideas of what Sergius would do. Our patriotism. Our heroic ideals. I sometimes used to doubt if they were anything but dreams. ... When I buckled on Sergius's sword ...

> it came into my head just as he was holding me in his arms and looking into my eyes, that perhaps we only had our heroic ideas because ... we were so delighted with the opera that season at Bucharest. Real life is so seldom like that! ... Only think ... I doubted him: I wondered whether all his heroic qualities and his soldiership might not prove mere imagination when he went into a real battle. ... Oh, to think that it was all true! ... that the world is really a glorious world for women who can see its glory and men who can act its romance!

Raina is left alone. Captain Bluntschli, a Serbian officer fleeing from Sergius's charge and looking for a place to hide, enters Raina's bedchamber. Raina's ideas of a soldier are upset by Bluntschli, who is afraid to die and who carries chocolate cream candies into battle in place of cartridges because they often prove more useful. Bluntschli informs Raina that Sergius came on in his cavalry charge "like an operatic tenor ... with flashing eyes and lovely moustache, shouting his war-cry" and that Sergius and all his men would have been slaughtered in this foolhardy charge had not the Serbs been sent the wrong-caliber ammunition. Raina replies,

> Oh, Captain Bluntschli, you are a very poor soldier: a chocolate cream soldier!

In Act II the romantic-anti-romantic theme is restated and further complicated. Sergius, the "hero of the hour," returns from the war to profess his high and lofty love for Raina.

> Dearest: all my deeds have been yours. You inspired me. I have gone through the war like a knight in a tournament with his lady looking down at him!

But this "higher" love fatigues Sergius, and behind the scenes he makes the lower kind of love to Louka, Raina's maid. Louka tells Sergius she has overhead Raina talking to Bluntschli:

> And I tell you ... Miss Raina will marry him. ... I know the difference between the sort of manner you and she put on before one another and the real manner.

In Act III, through reversals, antitheses, and parallels the theme is turned inside out and right side in. Sergius strikes an anti-romantic pose:

> Oh, war! war! the dream of patriots and heroes! A fraud, Bluntschli. A hollow sham, like love .... Life's a farce.

The realistic Louka, who from the beginning has seen through Sergius's "fictitious morals and fictitious good conduct," now uses them to capture him ("These heriocs ... have their practical side after all").

Bluntschli, who from the beginning has seen through Raina's posing, says to her,

> When you strike that noble attitude and speak in that thrilling voice, I admire you; but I find it impossible to believe a single word you say.

Raina, bored with the chivalrous Sergius, is captured by the unchivalrous Bluntschli. Beneath Raina's sham nobility, beneath her "romantic morality" is a "natural morality" which enables her to select the chocolate cream soldier as a mate. Bluntschli's "sagacity," it turns out, conceals a romantic attitude:

> And I . . . a man who has spoiled all his chances in life through an incurably romantic disposition. . . . I ran away from home twice when I was a boy. I went into the army instead of my father's business. I climbed the balcony of this house when a man of sense would have dived into the nearest cellar.

Bluntschli, it would appear, has "less sense than even" Sergius. But Bluntschli is responsive to the life force moving in Raina and is captured by what is not imagination, by Raina's youth and charm and consciousness.

The parts of the play are held together from the inside, "stitched internally," through the adherence of every detail to the theme. A series of contrasts between the romantic and the anti-romantic harmonizes parts and whole. The following diagram sketches a few of the ways in which the theme of *Arms and the Man* defines its structure.

---

romantic and anti-romantic attitudes and actions toward war, love, and life determine structure

ACT I

Raina is told about Sergius' charge

glorious . . . gallant . . . splendid	herioc ideals	
the hero of Slivnitza	noble attitudes	
the idol of the regiment	dreams	romantic
	imagination	
	lies	

Raina meets Bluntschli

a chocolate cream soldier	unheroic	
afraid to die	unconventional attitudes	anti-romantic
	realistic	
	true	

ACT II

Sergius returns to Raina

high love (fatiguing)	false manner	
Dearest	conventional attitudes	romantic
my deeds are yours	hypocrisy	

Louka and Sergius

low love (not so fatiguing)	realistic actions	
need for relief from high love	realistic attitudes	anti-romantic
stand back where we can't be seen	common sense	

ACT III

Sergius to Bluntschli

war a hollow sham
patriotism a sham
love a sham
life a sham

anti-romantic pose ⎫
overly dramatic attitudes ⎬ romantic

Bluntschli to Sergius

I spoiled my chances in life
I ran away from home
I climbed a balcony

realistic appraisal of ⎫
romantic self ⎬ anti-romantic
"truth" ⎭

Throughout Acts I, II, and III, reversals, transformations in Raina and Bluntschli's relation to theme:

Raina is romantic in Act I; in Act III she is thoroughly realistic in her response to Bluntschli's vitality.

Bluntschli appears unromantic in Act I; in Act III he reveals himself as an incurable romantic, yet realistically responds to Raina's "real" charm.

Throughout the three acts of the play the theme that "the tragedy and comedy of life lies in the consequence ... of ... our imaginations" is stated in action, character, and dialogue to expose our romantic attitudes toward war, love, and life. It is this theme, as it knits together all the materials of the play, that determines its structure.

Logical Structure

Parts of a work may cohere not so much by abstract idea or narrative action as **by logic;** that is, **parts may be held together by the binding power of statements or premises leading to a conclusion.**

Andrew Marvell's "To His Coy Mistress" provides one of the best-known examples of logical structure. By argumentation a lover attempts to convince his reluctant mistress that they should make love now. Each of the three parts of the poem presents a step in the argument. Stanza I begins,

> Had we but world enough, and time,
> This coyness, Lady, were no crime.

The lover then gives detail after detail to indicate how he would approach the lady *if* there were enough time and space to match the depth and expansiveness of his love:

> An hundred years should go to praise
> Thine eyes, and on they forehead gaze;
> Two hundred to adore each breast,
> But thirty thousand to the rest;
> An age at least to every part,
> And the last age should show your heart.
> For, Lady, you deserve this state,
> Nor would I love at lower rate.

Stanza II argues that there is not, however, "world enough, and time."

> But at my back I always hear
> Time's wingéd chariot hurrying near;
> And yonder all before us lie
> Deserts of vast eternity.

The speaker then gives detail after detail of what will occur if action is not taken:

> Thy beauty shall no more be found,
> Nor, in thy marble vault, shall sound
> My echoing song, then worms shall try
> That long-preserved virginity,
> And your quaint honor turn to dust,
> And into ashes all my lust.

Having indicated the high "rate" he would love at *if* there were "world enough, and time," and then having made it clear to his mistress that under the existing circumstances of life there is not world or time enough, the lover, in Stanza III, reasons that *therefore* they should love at a "lower rate."

> Now therefore, while the youthful hue
> Sits on thy skin like morning dew,
> And while thy willing soul transpires
> At every pore with instant fires,
> Now let us sport us while we may, . . .

In stanzas I, II, and III—through ironic and hyperbolic statements of the time and space requisite for the expression of his great love, through pictures of inactive confinement in eternity, and through images of the "sweetness" and "pleasures" to be had by seizing this present opportunity—the lover attempts to flatter, frighten, and arouse his mistress to the desired action. Taken together, the three stanzas present an argument (an if-but-therefore argument) which may be seen as still another attempt at seduction—this time by syllogism. The steps of the syllogism, it may be noted, serve not only as a means of convincing the lady but as a technique for structuring the major parts of the poem.

Emotional Structure

Emotion is, of course, inherent in all literature. But in some works **the pattern of emotions may**, more than any other aspect, **determine the arrangement of parts.** Thus, an author may have organized the parts of his work with the primary intention of communicating a particular emotional effect. The study of emotional structure is elusive and inexact because emotion in a work of literature is not single but multiple, and because the emotional effect of each part is to some extent derived, by way of parallels and contrasts, from its relationship with other parts. The following marking of William Butler Yeats's "The Second Coming" indicates one possible reading of the poem's structure.

I

(i)
[Turning and turning in the widening gyre
The falcon cannot hear the falconer;
(ii)
Things fall apart; the center cannot hold;
(iii)
Mere anarchy is loosed upon the world,
The blood-dimmed tide is loosed, and everywhere
The ceremony of innocence is drowned;
(iv)
The best lack all conviction, while the worst
Are full of passionate intensity.]

II

(a)
[Surely some revelation is at hand;
Surely the Second Coming is at hand.
The Second Coming!] **(b)** [Hardly are those words out
When a vast image out of Spiritus Mundi
Troubles my sight:] **(c)** [Somewhere in sands of the desert
A shape with lion body and the head of a man,
A gaze blank and pitiless as the sun,
Is moving its slow thighs, while all about it
Reel shadows of the indignant desert birds.]
(d) [The darkness drops again;] **(e)** [but now I know
That twenty centuries of stony sleep
Were vexed to nightmare by a rocking cradle.]
(f) [And what rough beast, its hour come round at last,
Slouches towards Bethlehem to be born?]

Stanza I describes the state of things in the present. Three images and a statement present what may appear to be a restrained description of the political and spiritual condition of man: the falcon and the falconer lose contact (i); the cohesive center of a centrifugal force gives way (ii); an inundation of mass confusion and disorder drowns ceremony, sensitivity, courtesy (iii); decent people are without belief, and indecent people are without doubt (iv). But beneath the surface appearance of controlled, objective description may be discerned a flood of anxiety, a cry of despair at the disintegration and dissolution of order and ceremony: "Every nerve trembles with horror at what is happening...."

The subject of stanza II is not the present but the future. History, as Yeats saw it, moves in cycles of 2,000 years. The present chaos and violence signals the end of the preceding age and ushers in the next age. Stanza II, which is an emotional response to stanza I, looks forward to the next 2,000 years.

The poet makes an emotional leap from the horror of the situation (stanza I) to hope, born out of despair, for the Second Coming of Christ (stanza II, part a). However painful and undesired it may be, Christ's judgment will resolve the present chaos and violence.

But at the moment the poet grasps for the anticipated Second Coming of Christ, he transcends himself to make contact with *Spiritus Mundi,* a supernatural, psychic storehouse of universal forces(b).

The image received from the Universal Spirit is given (c). The next coming is not Christ's. A rough shape with a "gaze blank and pitiless" is moving its "slow thighs" over the "sands of the desert" to be born.

The poet loses contact with the universal spirit (d). The image of the temper of the next age is gone.

But now the poet knows something about the relationship between past, present, and future (e). He knows that the preceding 2,000 years of Christianity, a period of "stony sleep," a cycle which began with Christ's "rocking cradle," will be followed by its opposite, by the nightmare symbolized in the oncoming "shape."[1]

"And what rough beast ... Slouches ... to be born (f)?" What terrifying age is this coming on us?

The emotion of the poem cannot be separated from theme, imagery, diction, and the other aspects of the work, but in a very general way it can be said that the arrangement of parts and the total emotional impact of the poem depend on its structure, on the pattern of its emotions, on the movement from indignant horror to desperate hope to frightful knowledge to terrified wonder.

Reading Techniques: Outlining the Relationship of Parts

Discerning parts, discovering their relationship, and understanding the relationship of each part to the whole are basic requirements in reading for structure. Following is an illustration of the technique of outlining the structure of a work to clarify the relationship between parts. The technique is an example of one way of studying structure, one way of beginning to see the work as a whole.

The structure of Henry James's "The Beast in the Jungle" is not primarily "logical" or "thematic" (James, it has been said, illustrates a "baffling escape from Ideas"). Nor does the structure grow out of the story's meager action, which leaves the reader with a sense that nothing has happened. More than narrative action, the story is a description and a dramatization of a motionless situation, of a stagnant relationship between two people.

After nearly ten years, John Marcher once again meets May Bartram. Marcher only vaguely remembers their first meeting and does not at all remember having told this woman the "secret" of his life: "His conviction, his apprehension, his obsession ... that something or other lay in wait for him, amid the twists and the turns of the months and the years, like a crouching beast in the jungle." May asks Marcher, "Isn't what you describe perhaps but the expectation ... of falling in love?" Marcher says it is not, that "*It*" is to be something much larger. Through the years Marcher keeps their relationship on the basis of their mutual interest in

---

[1]This is a difficult line and it has been interpreted in different ways. Perhaps the poet refers not to the 2,000 years A.D. but to the 2,000 years B.C.

his beast. Together they wait and watch for the beast to spring. Together they grow old. May becomes ill and dies. Marcher journeys about the world and then returns to London to make periodic visits to May's grave. One afternoon at her grave, Marcher sees the face of another man who is visiting another grave. The man's face is ravaged by pain, suffering, passion, love. Marcher suddenly realizes the nature of his beast.

This summary gives little indication of the organizing principle underlying the story. The structure of James's story (and of many modern stories) may be termed "psychological." "A psychological reason," James wrote, "is, to my imagination, an object adorably pictorial; to catch the tint of its complexion—I feel as if that idea might inspire one to Titianesque efforts. There are few things more exciting to me, in short, than a psychological reason." It is this "psychological reason," the "discovery" of the mystery of "poor" Marcher's self-centered being, that gives the story its structure.

James has divided "The Beast in the Jungle" into six parts, each containing a description, summary, and analysis of the situation and, also, one scene—that is, a passage of rendered action. In every part new facets of Marcher's consciousness are revealed by his reaction to a series of "warnings against egotism." Here is one possible outline, which serves to simplify and clarify the structure of the story.

Section I

Marcher: "I met you years and years ago in Rome. I remember all about it."

It hadn't been at Rome—it had been at Naples . . . he really didn't remember the least thing about her . . . the feeling of an occasion missed. . . .

May: "You said you had had from your earliest time, as the deepest thing within you, the sense of being kept for something rare and strange, possibly prodigious and terrible, that was sooner or later to happen to you, that you had in your bones the foreboding and the conviction of, and that would perhaps overwhelm you.

Marcher: "Then you will watch with me?" . . .
May: "I'll watch with you."
    [Marcher obsessed with his "beast," with the "sense of being kept for something." So obsessed with "my affair" that he is interested only in "the thing."]

Section II

Marcher . . . was careful to remember that she had, after all, also a life of her own, with things that might happen to her. . . .

It was one of his proofs to himself, the present he made her on her birthday, that he had not sunk into real selfishness.

May: "it isn't . . . the end of your watch. . . . You've everything still to see."

Marcher: "You know something I don't. . . . You know what's to happen."

    [Marcher imagines himself unselfish: he is "careful to remember" that May also has a life. Prides himself on his own sublime

102   Chapter Nine

unselfishness in his relation with her. May sees the beast. Marcher cannot see it because he sees with it—i.e., he looks out through his "eyeholes" with "the very eyes of the Beast."]

Section III

... the day came ... that his friend confessed to him her fear of a deep disorder in her blood. ...

⎱

Marcher ... immediately began ... to think of her peril as the direct menace for himself of personal privation.

⎱

... what was still first in his mind was the loss she herself might suffer. "What if she should have to die before knowing, before seeing—?"

⎱

... caught himself ... really wondering if the great accident would take form now as nothing more than his being condemned to see this charming woman, this admirable friend pass away from him.

[*Marcher reacts to May's impending death. The thought of it gives him a "chill," for he sees in it (i) his own personal privation, (ii) her loss—she will not be there to see his beast spring.*

Marcher fearful that what he is to "face" in life is nothing more than May's death. If this is all the beast is, it would not be "proportionate to the posture he has kept all his life." Hopes only that It will prove to be as large and unique as he has imagined it to be and not just this "charming" woman's death.]

Section IV

(May is dying.) Marcher: "What do you regard as the very worst that ... can happen to me?"

⎱

(May moves near Marcher, who is standing by the "chimney piece, fireless and squarely adorned.")

⎱

... he only waited. ... She turned off and regained her chair. ... It was the end of what she had been intending.

⎱

Marcher showed once more his mystification. "What then has happened?"

⎱

"What was *to," she said.*

[*Marcher asks May to tell him what she knows that he doesn't know. May moves to him, offering him a chance to "escape" his beast, a chance to feel, love, suffer, live, to give something of himself. Marcher waits for May to give him something more before she dies. The beast springs. Marcher does not know it has sprung.*]

Section V

She was dying, and his life would end. ... Her dying, her death, his consequent solitude—that was what he had figured as the beast in the jungle. ... He had lived by her aid, and to leave her behind .. What could be more overwhelming than that?

⎱

(May is buried in "the great grey London cemetery.")

... the Jungle had been threshed to vacancy and ... the Beast had stolen away.

... poor Marcher waded through his beaten grass, where no life stirred ... very much as if vaguely looking for the Beast, and still more as if missing it.

> [*Marcher senses he has missed the beast. Now without the "suspense" of "It" "to come," Marcher wanders "vaguely" in an existence extinct of It. But he continues to live with "his unidentified past."*]

Section VI

Asia ... the past glories of the Pharaohs were nothing to him ... he was but wondrous to himself. ...

The creature beneath the sod knew of his rare experience. ... Thus in short he settled to live—feeding only on the sense that he once had lived. ...

... the face of a fellow mortal ... a ... neighbor at the other grave ... nothing lived but the deep ravage of the feature ... scarred passion ... the raw glare of grief. ... What had the man had to make him, by the loss of it, so bleed and yet live?

No passion had ever touched Marcher ... something he had utterly, insanely missed ... she was what he had missed ... he had been the man, to whom nothing on earth was to have happened.

This horror of waking—this knowledge. ... He saw the Jungle of his life and saw the lurking Beast. ...

> [*Marcher believes he has lived, discovers he hasn't, and falls under the knowledge of "the chill of his egoism and the light of her use"—the "horror" of his unlived existence, the consciousness of his beast comes, after all these years, too late.*]

The structure of "The Beast in the Jungle" has grown out of the author's rendering of the egoism of the main character. Each of the six parts of the story gives a picture of progressively deeper stages of Marcher's consciousness. The way James chose to show this consciousness has determined the arrangement of the major parts of the story.

Writing Suggestions

When you write about the structure of a work, you will need to show how the major parts interact to shape the total work. The following questions may lead you to an understanding of the interaction of parts and to a topic for a paper on the structure of a work.

What are the major divisions?—five chapters? four quatrains and a couplet? ...

What is the subject of each of the major divisions?—decay, decay, decay, love? freedom from fear, freedom from fear, freedom from fear, fear? . . .

What is the emotion of each of the major divisions?—raving, indignant rebelliousness; meek, fearful submission? enthusiasm and confusion; bitterness and pain; understanding and comfort? . . .

Is there a dramatic reversal of emotion?—the word "but" marks a change from that which is positive and desirable to that which is negative and undesirable? takes an hour-glass shape: step by step we see a woman's growing attraction for a man; they are married (the hour glass is turned); step by step we see her increasing revulsion for her husband? . . .

Does the structure depend on a pattern of logic?—if . . . then; if . . . then; if . . . then; therefore? it could be this, it could be that, I think this, But If . . ., Then I think this? . . .

Is the structure emphasized by setting?—beginning: a deserted Indian well; middle: man enters and lives by the well; ending: the deserted well? the scaffold marks three high points in the story? . . .

Is the structure dependent on the action?—a murder is reported; the mob forms; they hunt for the murderers; they lynch the innocent men; the psychological reaction to the lynching? the old man searches for the fish, hooks him, fights him, kills him, battles the sharks, and returns with what remains of the fish? . . .

Before beginning to write your paper, decide what the major parts of the work are and how they are arranged. If *an abstract idea* is the dominant force behind the selection and arrangement of the parts, the body of your paper may be primarily an exposition of this idea as it manifests itself in each major part. If the parts cohere through the binding power of *a logical argument,* make clear the skeletal outline of the logic and the details that support each part of that argument. If *a pattern of emotion* determines the arrangement of parts, then you will need to discuss the nature of these emotions, indicating how one emotion leads into, parallels, or contrasts with another emotion to shape the total work.

In your paper you should clarify the major parts of the work you are writing about. You should also show how an idea, a logical argument, an emotional pattern or some other element of the work has determined its structure. You may then go one step further and interpret the special effects the structure of the work has achieved.

Theme, Thesis, and the Writing of a Critical Paper

THEME is not an aspect of literature in quite the same sense as are setting, character, plot, or any of the other aspects of literary study previously discussed. Two current definitions of the term "theme" are in common use and need to be distinguished.

According to one definition, **THEME is the "meaning," the view of life, embodied in the complex interrelation of all the various elements that shape and unify the total work.** Theme *is* the literary work and the literary work *is* the theme. "How can we know the dancer from the dance?" The dancer, in the act of dancing, is the dance; and the dance only exists as the dancer in the act of dancing it. Clearly, then, no abstract statement pinned on a work from outside is its "meaning," which can be stated only in the way in which it is.

According to the other definition, **"THEME" is the abstract subject of a work.** For example, the subject of "A Rose for Emily" (pp. 31-33) is, perhaps, the decadent past in conflict with the materialistic present. The subject of *The Iliad* (pp. 10-12) is anger growing out of pride or the nonacceptance of things. The subject of "Frankie and Johnny" (pp. 14-17) is the inconstancy of love. Theme used in this sense refers to recurring conditions of life as they affect human experience.

When writing a critical paper, you may find both definitions of "theme" useful —as the "meaning" *embodied in,* and inseparable from, the concrete details of a work; and as the abstract subject which may be perceived *emerging from* the concrete details of a work.

Not the theme of a work, however, but your **THESIS**, your assumption, about one of the work's essential "meanings" will provide the central idea for your paper. **A thesis statement, then, is the proposition you advance about the "theme" of the work; it is the controlling idea of your paper.**

A thesis statement about a work will necessarily grow out of your reading of such elements as character, plot, setting, point of view, style, tone, imagery, symbolism, structure — any of these approaches to a work may lead you to an understanding of one or a number of its many possible "meanings."

For example, approaching "A Rose for Emily" through setting, you might arrive at the idea that "Emily Grierson's house emphasizes the conflict between past and present: the decadent, but spirited and stubborn, Southern tradition as it asserts itself in its conflict with gross, Yankee materialism." Approaching *The Iliad* through character, you might advance the thesis that "The primary source of Achilleus' anger toward Agamemnon and Hektor is not their actions but Achilleus' inability to accept his fate." Approaching "Frankie and Johnny" through plot, you may want to show how "Frankie's shots, 'roota-toot-toot,' resolve the conflict between Johnny's vanity and Frankie's love."

Settling on a thesis is not always easy. You may find some preliminary steps to the actual formulation of a thesis helpful. First, decide on a **topic**; that is, **a fairly specific subject**. Next, you may need to *limit the topic to a still more specific subject,* one that you can handle in the prescribed space of a short critical paper. After you have limited your topic, it should be easier to formulate a thesis statement. The thesis statement will provide the central idea and will determine the objectives and the focus of your paper.

The two basic ingredients of a critical paper are thesis statement and support for it. These two ingredients call into action a particular mental process: (1) close reading of the concrete details of the work; (2) an idea, or thesis, about the "meaning" of those details; (3) a return to the concrete details for support for the thesis.

Once you have gone through this mental process of moving back and forth between concrete details and abstract idea, once you have committed yourself to a particular thesis and have found support for it, you may find that a tentative outline which organizes support for your thesis and clarifies the arrangement of the major parts of your paper will be a practical, if not always necessary, step in the writing of your paper.

Following is an illustration of one method for preparing a critical paper. The proposed paper on Katherine Mansfield's short story "Bliss" approaches the story primarily through a study of character, though the Reading Techniques discussed under *Point of View* and *Tone* (Irony) could also have been the basis for the thesis statement and the outline that follow. The discussion of "Bliss" given on pages 37–38 should provide you with sufficient information for understanding what is given below.

Preparing a Critical Paper

Selecting a topic
   "Bliss"—a study in self-delusion

Limiting the topic
   "Bliss"—a study not of bliss but of imagination, a study of a continuous and impenetrable self-delusion

Formulating a thesis statement
   In Katherine Mansfield's "Bliss" the main character, Bertha Young, believes she is joyously alive, radiantly happy, but, in reality, she lives in a stringent, screaming prison of self-delusion.

Outlining support for the thesis statement

Introduction { *Bertha's relation to (1) her own emotional state, (2) the guests who come to her party, (3) her husband and Miss Fulton and their affair. Each relationship makes clear the gap between what Bertha believes to be true and what is, in fact, true.*

Body {

I. Bertha's relation to herself
   A. Bertha believes she is filled with "absolute bliss."
      1. Bertha wants to dance and laugh . . . "at nothing" . . . feels the "fire of bliss . . . blazing—blazing."
      2. She feels as if she has swallowed a "bright piece of sun."
   B. Bertha's "bliss" is more akin to hysteria than bliss.
      1. When Bertha looks into the "cold mirror" we see a woman . . . "with smiling, trembling lips."
      2. Bertha laughs—she is on the verge of becoming "hysterical": "Bertha had to dig her nails into her hands—so as not to laugh too much."

II. Bertha's relation to her guests
   A. Bertha believes they are "modern, thrilling friends . . . dears—dears."
      1. She thinks the Norman Knights "a very sound couple."
      2. She adores Eddie Warren—"a most attractive person."
   B. Bertha's friends are more ridiculous than they are "sound" and "attractive."
      1. The Knights call each other "Face" and "Mug" and speak of things as being "creamy."
      2. Eddie Warren says his white stockings have gotten "so much whiter since the moon rose."

III. Bertha's relation to her husband and to Pearl Fulton
   A. Bertha believes she loves both of them.
      1. "Oh, she loved him" . . . Harry "had such a zest for life" . . . Bertha "understood."
      2. Bertha "always did fall in love with beautiful women" . . . Miss Fulton is "wonderful, wonderful" . . . Bertha thinks she understands Miss Fulton "perfectly."
   B. Bertha's relation to Harry and Miss Fulton is imaginary.
      1. Bertha and Harry have often talked about how cold she, Bertha, is to him.
      2. In the hall Bertha sees Harry whispering "I adore you" to Miss Fulton and arranging a liaison for the next day. Bertha's reaction to the affair reflects her inability to see and to respond to reality: Bertha runs to the window, "'Oh, what is going to happen now?' she cried."

Conclusion
> *Bertha does not distinguish her own stringent, hysterical emotions from "bliss."*
> *Bertha does not see that her friends are not "modern," "thrilling," and "delightful" but false and ridiculous.*
> *Bertha does not realize that her feelings for Harry and Miss Fulton are based on the imaginary pictures she has of these two people. Nor does she perceive Harry's and Miss Fulton's feelings for her—nor their feelings for each other.*
> *From the beginning of the story Bertha believes that her whole world is "good," is "right": "All that happened seemed to fill again her brimming cup of bliss."*
> *Her world is not the way she imagines it.*

The method of preparation suggested above—of finding a topic, limiting it, formulating a thesis statement, and outlining material—is a somewhat formal way of getting started. Another way to begin is to plunge directly into the writing of your paper, discovering thesis and organization in the activity of writing. This method—or lack of method—may require several preliminary drafts, but, depending on the way your mind works, it may prove just as suitable.

Whichever method you use, your objective should be to do one or both of the following: (1) give new insights into the work you are writing about for your reader, who has not read it as carefully as you have; (2) give support for an original and controversial idea that you have formulated about the work.

No matter what your objective, you should attempt to bring out the essential quality of the work. As one writer has said, "the lifeblood of the poetic creation is everywhere the same." Whether you tap a literary work at character, plot, setting, point of view, style, tone, imagery, symbolism, or structure, try to penetrate to the life of the work. Through the application of the techniques at your command, you should now be preapred, when reading a work of literature and writing about it, to make your own tapping of its lifeblood.

Writing Exercises

Writing about your own experiences is somewhat different, of course, from writing a critical paper about a literary work, for you are dealing directly with the elusiveness of experience itself. The following exercises point you to your own feelings, thoughts, opinions, ideas—not to an analysis and interpretation of someone else's.

Here are a few general suggestions for writing about your experience:

Write about what you know: events you have lived through, actions you have performed, emotions you have felt, ideas you have thought, something your have undergone or observed first hand.

Do not try to say it all. Select a point of focus. Zero in on one thing and do it justice.

Let concrete details add up to an abstract idea. Or, to put it another way, let an abstract idea govern concrete details. This, of course, requires that you know the "meaning" of the experience you are writing about.

Rework the first draft of everything you like, paying special attention to word choice (p. 46) and sentence structure (p. 49).

If you are having trouble getting started, just start. Write freely. Consider details, focus, organization, diction later. The next day, if you like what you have done and feel it merits it, rework it, polish it up.

The following exercises are not meant to confine you to writing about prescribed topics but to suggest experiences out of your own life as material for composition. The exercises are, then, suggestions—not questions to be answered or assignments to be followed.

No length has been set down for an exercise. Your response to the exercise can determine the length of your paper—whether it be a paragraph, 300 words, 1,200, or longer. Let the content you discover for an exercise determine its length. The page numbers in the exercises refer to literary examples used in the previous nine chapters.

1. Take notes on someone who is continually pushing one opinion they have of themselves. Write a paper focusing on this one psychological quirk. Give quotes ("I was born in a ditch," p. 1) to illustrate.
2. Narrate an incident in your life that shows different sides of your character: you expected one thing and acted one way; you got something other than you expected, and reacted. You might dramatize the incident by putting down different things you said, setting off the small, humble word ("Pray you undo this little button," for example, p. 3) with the large, dramatic shout ("Rumble thy belly full," p. 2).
3. Do you know someone like Pangloss (p. 3) who believes an idea to such an extent that he or she blissfully refuses to see the realities at his or her feet that contradict it? Try to get the idea and the person down on paper.
4. Write a description of someone who emotionally resembles Katerina Ivanovna (p. 4), who desires harmony or peace to such an extent that she or he flies into a fit at the slightest discord or makes war to save the peace.
5. Present a love scene so that the characters of the two lovers emerge from what they say ("Say you love me." "I reckon that's what ails me, Madge," p. 5).
6. Put down on paper some thoughts that you keep hidden from others. Yours are, perhaps, different from Richard's ("I am determined to prove a villain," p. 6).
7. Make clear your beliefs about how your "God" acts in relation to man or, for example, sea-crabs ("two worms for the sea-crab whose nippers end in red," p. 7).
8. Define hate or cruelty by illustrating it in action ("the raw face came crashing across the table toward her, howling . . . ," p. 8).
9. Express the distaste you have felt for some rich, proud person ("fine, tall person, handsome features . . . till his manners gave a disgust," p. 9).
10. Give an example of nonchalance, either natural or affected (Hopalong: "At first I reckoned mebby it might be an old one," p. 10).
11. Show how pride may be the basis for rage, self-pity, or sorrow ("Achilleus/Weeping went and sat in sorrow," p. 10).

12. Discuss the idea of justice or of double standards in the male-female relationship ("There was her lovin' Johnny a-lovin' up Alice Fry," p. 15).
13. Describe an event that changed in some one way your outlook on life (after the journey through the woods Goodman is "a stern, and sad, a darkly meditative, a distrustful man," p. 19).
14. Have you known someone whose life has passed "drearily without warmth" (p. 21)? Discuss the causes of a dull existence and the things that are required for a full life.
15. Write about a time in your life when you were caught between two undesirable forces. It may not, of course, be as dramatic as Odysseus sailing between Scylla and Charybdis (p. 25). Maybe there was a time when you were trying to avoid a little work and you ended up having to do a great deal. Or perhaps there was a time in your life when you had to decide whether to go or to stay, to act or not to act—while desiring neither alternative.

16. *Describe the streets of a city you know. Let the details ("old women whose hair is full of the blood of ticks," p. 26, for example) add up to an overall impression ("the incubation of a human misery").*
17. *Compare the sun to something unusual ("Like an orange in a fried fish soup" p. 26).*
18. *Describe a person and the house he or she lives in so that the two, inhabitant and habitat, tortoise and shell, produce one effect ("chilling and depressing," for example, p. 29).*
19. *Describe two people, emphasizing the differences betwen them (Emily is "small and spare" and quiet; Homer big and loud, p. 31).*
20. *Describe a place so that the details you give ("a small cabin ... of clay and wattles made," p. 34) reveal the dominant feeling you have for it.*
21. *Capture on paper an emotion you had while on your way to a party, dance, or "happening." Make clear where you were when you had the emotion ("chill air and crowded closeness of the swaying carriage," p. 36), and what you imagined the happening would be like ("music, flowers, dance ... ").*
22. *What is the effect of death or war on you ("the possibility of suffering and death ... ," p. 36)?*
23. *Discuss the cause of wars. Argue for or against Tolstoy's position that Napoleon had no more power or force or control over the war than did the common footsoldier (p. 36).*
24. *Write about a time in your life when you felt "joy and strength in life" (p. 37) but were, paradoxically, miserable physically.*
25. *Describe your friends. Are they, for example, "modern thrilling friends" (p. 37)? What does your description of them tell you about yourself?*
26. *Relate a common activity of one of your parents and your reaction to it. The activity need not be so dramatic as "delirium tremens" (p. 39).*
27. *Try writing a passage of stream of consciousness. Begin by putting down on paper anything that comes into your mind in any order it comes in ("tripe ... afloat in the dead sea ... cracking knuckles ... ," p. 40).*
28. *Reconstruct a moment in your life when you realized some unknown deficiency or strength in yourself. Anchor the experience to a word ("The horror! The horror!" p. 43).*
29. *How do you think you will feel about your youth once it is gone ("Let go, farewell," p. 45)?*
30. *Describe a couple you know that make a dramatic contrast (a "soft sly slim slip," a "heavy trudging lurching," p. 47). Or compare and contrast male and female elements.*
31. *Write an autobiographical piece that doesn't begin "I was born in the year ... " (p. 49).*
32. *Write three loose, three periodic, and three balanced sentences (p. 49-51).*
33. *Write a sentence modeled after Hamlet's disjunctive style ("if ... , then ... ; if ... ; then ... ; if ... , then ... ," p. 52).*
34. *Present a dialogue between two people using an analogy to describe a climactic statement ("But in my ears it seemed as if somewhere the bell of death was ringing," p. 57).*

35. Describe a season of the year in two different paragraphs so that the tone of one passage is in opposition to the tone of the other ("sweet showers—cruelest pain," p. 58).
36. Analyze the double (or multiple) meanings of the last piece of verbal irony you heard or read (see p. 60).
37. Have you ever felt that someone did not "see," did not "know" you but instead only "saw" or "knew" what he imagined you to be? Describe the effect that this had on you ("You ache with the need to convince yourself that you do exist," p. 61).
38. Describe a time in your life when you were expecting something, or were dreaming that something very fine would happen and something not at all fine actually happened ("Hoity-toity!" p. 62).
39. Give the steps of some activity you have performed so that the reader can visualize the process ("washed...picked...packed ...covered...," p. 68).
40. Describe something which once gave you joy but now seems dull and lifeless ("Look for You Yesterday, Here You Come Today," p. 68).
41. Give your idea of the nature of modern man ("We are the hollow men...," p. 69).
42. Define melancholy ("...brooding Darkness," p. 69); indicate how it differs from morbidity. Give an example of it.
43. Give a satirical argument in defense of a belief you have or an emotion you hold for some person ("who says my tears...," p. 69).
44. Begin a paper with the sentence, "I should have been a _____" (for example, "a pair of ragged claws," p. 71). How do you think that what you think you should have been will influence what you will become?
45. Define faith. Discuss your "faith" in powers above man, or your "faith" in the future. Would you say your "faith" is "full and bright" or "retreating" (p. 73)?
46. Recall your reaction to a time when you felt "the weariness, the fever, and the fret" (p. 74) of this world. Did you think the solution lay in retiring from the world or in becoming more involved in it?
47. Compare and contrast physical and spiritual love ("But we by a love so much refined...," p. 76). Do you see the two as mutually exclusive—or does one grow, necessarily, out of the other?
48. Can valid opinion be based on feeling alone ("But that is what I feel," p. 80)? Argue the case for an opinion based on feeling or one based on thinking. When you have made major decisions in your life were they based primarily on feeling or on thinking?
49. Describe a leaf ("a leaf, only a leaf," p. 80).
50. Take a stand for or against an individual's freedom to be a sexual deviant. At what point does the individual's freedom infringe on the rights of others ("But at last he will shed his leaves," p. 81)?

Writing Exercises

51. Compare and contrast one thing that for you symbolizes the past (a tree "in its utmost fingers tenderness," p. 81) with one thing that symbolizes the present ("electric lights...sizzled and jagged," p. 81).

52. Describe the weather so that it reinforces an opinion you have about the university "system," government bureaucracy, student protest marches... ("...at the very heart of the fog, sits the Lord High Chancellor in his High Court," p. 82).

53. What is the nature of man? Is he "always in flight...by no joy sated" (p. 84), always aspiring to higher things, or is he lazy and continually thrusting "his nose into every filth" (p. 84)?

54. Is adventure, in your opinion, hollow? Is it without a "kernel" (p. 85)? State what you want from life and how you think adventure could help you get it.

55. Have you ever been like "Pliable" (p. 88)? Describe a situation in which you gave up your goal and give your reasons then for doing so.

56. Write out an argument for or against "freedom of the will"; that is, is man a "canary chittering feebly" (p. 90) in a cage or a full-throated bird in flight?

57. Look up the etymology of the word "virtue" (p. 93). Write a paper on its origin and history. Or indicate the meaning the word has for you.

58. Analyze a passage from a book, from a speech, or from a conversation, making clear why you "find it impossible to believe a single word" of it (p. 96).

59. Give an if-but-therefore argument (p. 97) persuading someone to act as you wish him or her to.

60. What do you imagine the future to be—a "rough beast" (p. 99) or utopia? How do you plan to prepare for this imagined future?

61. Distinguish between love and self-love ("he was but wondrous to himself," p. 103). Do you think men are more often victims of self-love than women and women more often victims of vanity than men?

62. Relate one thing that you feel you have "missed" in your life ("She was what he had missed," p. 103).

Selected Analytic Cross-Reference Chart

Almost any work of literature, as has often been noted, can be approached in many different ways. This chart lists works which seem appropriate to an approach other than the one taken in this book. You may use it in two ways: (1) to exercise your understanding of the aspects of literary study previously discussed, (2) to find a suitable approach for writing a critical paper on a work that was of particular interest to you.

For example, you may want to test your understanding of IMAGERY. To do so you might turn, as is suggested in the chart, to the quotation from *The Horse's Mouth* (p. 26). This quotation has been discussed from the standpoint of setting, but it contains imagery which you may now discover and analyze with the reading techniques at your command.

Or you may be in search of a topic for a paper and, remembering that the character of Huck Finn interested you as it was shown in the passage quoted from *Huckleberry Finn* under POINT OF VIEW (p. 39), you could turn to the complete novel and write a paper, not on the point of view of *Huckleberry Finn* but on the character of Huck.

By using this chart in the ways suggested, you may come to see a work of literature from more than one angle and to make more and more connections between elements within it.

Character
Père Goriot (p. 29-31)
"Young Goodman Brown" (p. 19-21)
War and Peace (p. 35-37)
Huckleberry Finn (p. 39-40)
Hamlet (p. 60-61)

Plot

Candide (p. 3-4)
"Bliss" (p. 37-39)
Agamemnon (p. 63)
A Farewell to Arms (p. 81-82)
Arms and the Man (p. 94-97)

Setting

"In the Cart" (p. 21-23)
"The Lake Isle of Innisfree" (p. 34)
"The Fiend" (p. 80-82)
Howards End (p. 81-82)
The Pilgrim's Progress (p. 88)

Point of View

"A Rose for Emily" (p. 31-33)
Justine (p. 25-26)
"The Love Song of J. Alfred Prufrock" (p. 71)
Bleak House (p. 82-83)
"The Beast in the Jungle" (p. 100-103)

Style

The Canterbury Tales (p. 58-59)
"The Waste Land" (p. 58-59)
The Sun Also Rises (p. 67-68)
"L'Allegro" (p. 69)
"Ode to a Nightingale" (p. 73-74)

Tone

Hard Times p. (p. 1-3)
Richard III (p. 6)
Finnegans Wake (p. 47-48)
"To His Coy Mistress" (p. 97-98)
"Virtue" (p. 93-94)

Imagery

The Horse's Mouth (p. 26-27)
"Sailing to Byzantium" (p. 28-29)
"Caliban upon Setebos" (p. 6-7)
Faust (p. 83-84)
"Peer Gynt" (p. 85)

Symbolism

King Lear (p. 2-3)
"The Collar" (p. 47)
"The Hollow Men" (p. 69)
"Dover Beach" (p. 73)
"The Second Coming" (p. 98-100)

Structure

"Frankie and Johnny" (p. 14-17)
Heart of Darkness (p. 41-43)
Jude the Obscure (p. 62)
"A Valediction Forbidding Mourning" (p. 75-77)
McTeague (p. 88-91)

Glossary and Index of Literary Terms

ABSTRACT, a term used to describe words or statements which represent ideas or generalities; opposed to **CONCRETE,** a term used to describe words or statements which represent particular persons, places, or things.

Some words are more abstract than others: "wearing apparel" is more abstract (more general) than "scarlet red hose" which is more concrete (more particular). Not only words but statements lie along a scale of abstraction. "Man is not without blemishes" is higher on the scale of abstraction than "Upon the ridge of the Miller's nose was a wart and on it stood a tuft of hairs as red as the bristles in an old sow's ear." The philosophical expression tends to be abstract; the poetic, concrete.

ALLEGORY, an extended narrative in the form of an elaborate metaphor in which ideas or concepts are represented by characters and their actions. For a discussion of allegory see pp. 87-88.

ALLITERATION, the repetition of the same initial consonant sound in two or more words or in two or more syllables of a word. For example see p. 47.

ANAPEST. See **METER.**

ANTAGONIST, a character in a drama or narrative who opposes the protagonist. See **PROTAGONIST.**

ANTI-PLOT, MODERN. See Chapter 2, pp. 21-23.

ANTITHESIS, a device for emphasizing contrasting words, clauses, sentences, or ideas by putting them in parallel grammatical structure: "When attacked, the dragon bellows; when ignored, he preens his scales." See pp. 50-51.

ARCHETYPE, images, character types, or narrative structures which recur in literary works (as well as in myths and dreams) and which arise out of the "primordial" emotions slumbering in man's unconscious.

One of the most common archetypes is the rebirth archetype. E. M. W. Tillyard in *The Miltonic Setting Past and Present,* describes it as a pattern of "death, sorrow, the futility of ambition . . . ; the desire to escape them; acceptance of them in the end; and following it, renewed vitality." This archetypal theme of death and rebirth has been discovered by critics in such diverse places as the Biblical account of Jonah and the whale, Milton's "Lycidas," and Coleridge's *The Rime of the Ancient Mariner.*

ASSONANCE, the similarity of vowel sounds but the dissimilarity of the succeeding consonant sounds in the stressed syllables of two or more words. For examples see p. 48.

BALLAD, a short narrative poem originally designed to be sung. Ballads tell a story simply and directly through dialogue and described action. The most common stanza form is a four-line stanza (a quatrain) of alternating lines of iambic tetrameter and iambic trimeter, rhyming *abcb.*

BLANK VERSE, unrhymed iambic pentameter. More than any other verse form, blank verse comes closest to the natural rhythms of the English language. It has come to be used very frequently, especially for long, serious poetry. See **METER, RHYTHM.**

CATASTROPHE, the outcome or conclusion of a drama or narrative. The term is usually reserved for the denouement of a tragedy. See **DENOUEMENT** and **TRAGEDY.** See also pages 16-17.

CHARACTER, See Chapter 1, pp. 1 ff.

CLIMAX, (1) the high point of the reader's emotional response to a narrative or drama. See pp. 16, 22. (2) When used to describe the structure of a drama, climax is the decisive turning point, usually the moment of highest tension, when the fortunes of the main character change, the point at which rising action becomes falling action. In this sense the term is synonymous with crisis. See p. 17.

CLOSED COUPLET. See **COUPLET.**

COMEDY, broadly, any literary work that amuses us and ends happily. The tone of comedy is more often light than heavy, more often diverting or gay than grim and frightening. In Greek drama, comedy is represented by a mask with the corners of the mouth turned up. The term is elastic, however, and little can be said about it that is true in all cases.

Different types of comedy are commonly distinguished. (1) *Low comedy* makes use of clownish activity, coarse jokes, boisterous talk. It is opposed to (2) *high comedy*, which appeals to the intellect by exposing the folly and pretentions of human nature. The characters of high comedy, unlike those of low comedy, are usually sufficiently intelligent to perceive the weaknesses in others and in themselves. (3) In *romantic comedy* the main characters are lovers caught in love intrigues which are happily resolved at the end of the play with the suitable lovers united. (4) The *comedy of manners* or *social comedy* is concerned with revealing the artificial conventions of sophisticated society.

These are only a few of many different kinds of comedy; the line dividing any two of them is not sharp. High comedy, for example, often uses the devices of low comedy, and romantic comedy may, like the comedy of manners, expose the social absurdities of sophisticated society.

COMPLICATION, that part of a plot in which the problems or tensions caused by two opposing forces are developed. See pp. 15, 17.

CONCEIT, a comparison of two quite dissimilar things to draw an elaborate and striking parallel between them. See John Donne's "A Valediction Forbidding Mourning," pp. 75-77.

CONCRETE. See **ABSTRACT.**

CONFLICT, a struggle between two opposing forces. See discussion of **PLOT,** pp. 16-17, 22-23.

CONNOTATION, the implications of a word or the emotional associations that accompany it. See pp. 46-47, 59.

CONVENTION, broadly (1) any customary literary device or (2) recurring subject which is treated in an established way by different authors.

According to the first meaning of the term, a convention is any device commonly used by authors and accepted by audience or readers which provides a solution to an artistic problem; for example, the audience watching a play accepts the lowering and raising of the curtain to signify a passage of time within the context of the play.

According to the second meaning of the term, convention is the code, or body of rules, associated with a particular subject or situation. Two of the best known conventions are the *courtly love* and the *Petrarchan. Courtly love* (popular during the Middle Ages) follows these rules: a man must be deeply in love with a lady; the lady must not be his wife; the man wants to make love to her, not only for the pleasure of it, but also to come in touch with such abstract ideals as beauty and truth, and, ironically, morality; the lady does not readily accept him; the man suffers greatly: loses his appetite, trembles, turns pale, sighs, weeps, and can't sleep; if and when the lady ceases to ignore him, the man immediately regains his health. For a satiric treatment of this convention, see the lines from stanza II of John Donne's "The Canonization," p. 69.

In the *Petrarchan convention* a love-sick man laments a beautiful lady's indifferent response to his great love. The Petrarchan lover expresses, plaintively, pleadingly, his love for the lady by giving a catalogue of her features, describing each with exaggerated comparisons: the brightness of her eyes is like the sun; the redness of her lips and cheeks like coral or roses or rubies; her breasts, white as snow; her hair, fine golden wires; her breath, perfume; her voice, soft music....

COSMIC IRONY. See **IRONY,** also pp. 62-63.

COUPLET, two successive rhyming lines of verse, usually of the same meter. Formally, the couplet is a stanza of two lines. If both grammatical structure and thought are complete within the two lines, it is called a **CLOSED COUPLET.** If the couplet is in iambic pentameter it is a **HEROIC COUPLET.**

CRISIS, the decisive incident which marks the turning point of the protagonist's fortunes, either for better or for worse. The term is applied only to the arrangement of elements within a work and not, as is *climax,* to the reader's or spectator's emotional response. See pages 16-17.

DACTYL. See **METER.**

DENOTATION, the explicit meaning, or the express definition of a word. See pp. 46-47. See **CONNOTATION.**

DENOUEMENT, the outcome of the conflict in a plot. Denouement means, in addition, the final unraveling, or untying of the threads, the explanation of the ramifications of the plot in drama or fiction. See pp. 16-17.

DIALOGUE, a conversation between two or more persons. For an example see pp. 5-6.

DICTION, the way an author selects and arranges words. For a discussion, see pp. 46-48.

DISJUNCTION, the splitting of groups of words into two parts. See p. 52.

DRAMA, in its most general sense, any work meant to be performed on the stage by actors before an audience. A drama usually tells a story by means of dialogue and action. See **COMEDY, TRAGEDY.**

DRAMATIC IRONY. See **IRONY,** see also p. 63.

DRAMATIC MONOLOGUE, a poem in which one person, in a particular situation, sometimes addressing himself to another person, reveals his private thoughts and emotions. For a discussion of this term, see pp. 6-7.

DRAMATIC STRUCTURE, the arrangement and inherent relationships among the elements of a drama. See **CATASTROPHE, CLIMAX, CRISIS, DENOUEMENT, EXPOSITION, FALLING ACTION, RISING ACTION.** For a discussion of these terms see Chapter 2, **PLOT,** pp. 15-17.

ELEGY, in modern usage, a poem in which the poet laments the death of a particular person. Many elegies follow a pattern: The speaker expresses his sorrow over the person's death, reflects philosophically on death, and closes with a somber affirmation and acceptance of death.

EPIC, a long narrative poem focusing on the actions of a heroic figure. The action is sufficiently vast in scope and significance to affect a whole nation or civilization or to express its values and beliefs. See the discussion of *The Iliad* pp. 10-12, and the description of one of Beowulf's heroic feats, p. 70.

ESSAY, a composition dealing with a restricted topic, usually attempting a "study" of some subject and written to persuade the reader to a certain point of view. Unlike "creative" literature it is not an imaginative re-creation of reality but an interpretation of it.

A distinction is often made between the *informal* and the *formal* essay. The *informal essay* is personal, familiar, even intimate and chatty, perhaps. The author often uses private experiences and observations, sometimes humorously, to bring the reader into his confidence. The author's intention may be as much to express his own unique temperament, or to entertain the reader with a graceful, winning style, as it is to communicate his attitude toward a subject. The *formal essay* is impersonal, often sober, even dignified. It may be organized according to overt, logical argument with the primary object being to convince the reader of the importance and soundness of a particular idea. See, for example, the passage from Alexander Pope's *Essay On Man*, p. 51. Because this "essay" is written in verse, it is an exception to the prose style of almost all other essays.

EXPOSITION, the part of a plot which gives the necessary information in preparation for the events that are to follow. See pp. 15, 17.

FALLING ACTION, that part of the action of a dramatic plot following the climax, the resolution. See pp. 16-17.

FIGURE OF SPEECH, generally, an expression using words in nonliteral senses. For discussion and examples see pp. 68-70.

FIRST-PERSON POINT-OF-VIEW, See Chapter 4, **POINT OF VIEW,** pp. 39-40.

FLAT CHARACTER. See Chapter 1, **CHARACTER,** pp. 1-3.

FORESHADOWING, a hint of what is to happen later in a work. A raven, wolf, and vulture awaiting a battle foreshadow the deaths of brave men.

FREE VERSE, verse "freed" from the restrictions of a definite meter or line length. Though its metrical pattern is more irregular than conventional verse, its cadence or rhythmical movement is more uniform than ordinary prose.

GENRE, a term which signifies a "kind" or "type" of literary form. For example, tragedy, epic, lyric, comedy, and novel are different "kinds" of literary works. Many critics today think that the classification of works of literature into genres is often arbitrary and, in many cases, of little value.

HEROIC COUPLET. See **COUPLET.**

HYPERBOLE. See **OVERSTATEMENT.**

IAMB. See **METER.**

IMAGE CLUSTER, one image or a number of different images which are so interfused with the meaning of the work that an awareness of them is central to an understanding of the total work. See p. 75.

IMAGERY. See Chapter 7, pp. 67 ff.

IRONY, a disparity or discrepancy between statement and meaning, a means of making actuality (or what is meant) more dramatic by contrasting it with appearance (or what is not meant). In all irony there are two incongruous elements: for example, statement and fact, assumption and reality, the sublime and the ridiculous, illusion and actuality, or belief and truth.

There are different kinds of irony. In **VERBAL IRONY** (pp. 60-61) the speaker says the opposite of what he intends; his statement carries a double meaning. In **SITUATIONAL IRONY** (pp. 61-62) a circumstance or a series of events bring into existence contrasting elements. In **COSMIC IRONY** (pp. 62-63) the author's belief about the nature of things is in contrast with, for example, the character's belief about the way things are. In **DRAMATIC IRONY** (pp. 63-64) the audience knows what is happening, has happened, or will happen; the character does not.

LEITMOTIF, "leading motif," a recurring element within a single literary work—sometimes termed "motif." In Marcel Proust's *Rememberance of Things Past,* a "little phrase" from a violin sonata is heard and then, again and again, in different situations in different ways, reappears. The total work, as E. M. Forster points out, "hangs together because it is stitched internally" with such recurring elements as this "little phrase." See **MOTIF.**

LITOTES, a figure of speech, a form of understatement in which the speaker affirms something by saying the negative of its opposite. That is, instead of saying, "That was a crushing blow," the speaker, so as to attain a special effect, may say, "That was not a light tap." Thus, the speaker affirms that it was a heavy blow by saying that it was not a light tap. See also **UNDERSTATEMENT.**

LYRIC, a poem on any one particular subject expressing one person's emotions or thoughts. In a lyric the poet is not telling a story but capturing, or recapturing, a special moment, a private feeling, a frame of mind, or an idea. The speaker in the poem, it may be noted, is not necessarily always the poet himself but may be an invented character. The lyric, moreover, may be written in almost any form. Ballads, elegies, odes, and sonnets are types of lyrics. Generally, however, the lyric is short, emotional, and subjective, and often melodic, reflecting the origin of the form as a poem to be accompanied by music played on a lyre. See the discussion of William Butler Yeats's "The Lake Isle of Innisfree," pp. 34 ff.

MEIOSIS, understatement used for emphasis, humorous effect, or the purpose of belittling the subject. Closely related to **LITOTES** (p. 70). See also **UNDERSTATEMENT,** page 70.

METAPHOR, a figure of speech in which the comparison is not directly expressed but is implied. For discussion and example, see p. 69.

METER, the regular pattern of rhythm in a line of verse. In English, rhythm is based on accent. If a syllable is accented, it is said to be stressed (′); if unaccented, unstressed (˘). A metrical unit, or metrical foot, is a specified number of stressed and unstressed syllables. One of two ways of describing meter is to indicate the *number* of metrical feet a line contains:

one foot—monometer	five feet—pentameter
two feet—dimeter	six feet—hexameter
three feet—trimeter	seven feet—heptameter
four feet—tetrameter	eight feet—octameter

The other way of describing meter is to indicate the *kind* of metrical feet a line contains. The following poem by Samuel Taylor Coleridge illustrates each of these metrical feel:

Tróchĕĕ [ˊ˘] trĭps frŏm lońg tŏ shórt.
From long to long in solemn sort
Slów Spóndee [ˊˊ] stálks: strŏng fóot! yet ill able
Evĕŕ tŏ cóme ŭp wĭth Dáctyĭ trĭsyĭ́lăblĕ [ˊ˘˘].
Ĭaḿbĭcs [˘ˊ] márch frŏm shórt tŏ lońg.
Wĭth ă lĕap ańd ă boúnd thĕ swĭft Ánăpešts [˘˘ˊ] thróng.

Though it would be a mistake to associate definite emotions with each meter, different meters (depending, of course, on the author's handling of them) do move, as Coleridge suggests, in such a way as to carry different tonal qualities with them.

Iambic, the most common metrical foot in English, seems to march, or at least to go rather swiftly, as in this line: | Tŏ strĭ́ve, | tŏ séek, | tŏ fínd, | ańd nót | tŏ yiéld. |

Trochaic, the opposite of iambic, may be slow and solemn: | Thére thĕy | arĕ, mў | fíftў | mén ańd | wómĕn. |

Anapestic often seems to leap and bound as in: | Lĭke ă chĭ́ld | frŏm thĕ woḿb, | lĭke ă ghóst | frŏm thĕ toḿb. |

Dactylic sometimes has a strange, almost eerie quality: | Thĭ́s ĭs thĕ | fórešt prĭ | ḿevăl/ Thĕ | múrmŭrĭńg | pĭ́nes ańd thĕ | hémlŏčks. |

Spondaic is often slow and stalking and is used rarely, mainly as a substitute in a line of different meter. In the following line a spondaic foot has been used in place of the regular iambic foot: | Thĕ harĕ | lĭ́mped trém | blĭ́ng thróugh | thĕ fró | zĕn gráss. |

Thus, meter may emphasize emotion. This is not, of course, to imply that it is the meter rather than the pressure of the poet's thought and emotions lying behind the meter that determines the emotional quality of the poem. The poet does not rigidly follow a uniform metrical pattern but varies metrical foot and line length to reflect and reinforce the mood and sense of the poem.

Meter, it should be remembered, is only one of the many elements of poetry. See **RHYTHM, RHYME.**

METONYMY, a figure of speech in which something associated with a subject is used in its place. For an example, see p. 64.

MOTIF, a term usually applied to a situation or an idea which frequently recurs in literature. Two of the most common motifs are the **ubi sunt** ("where are they?") and the **carpe diem** ("seize the day").

In the **ubi sunt** motif, the speaker laments the passage of life as it is carried away by time. The motif occurs in two such widely different kinds of literature as Dante Gabriel Rossetti's "The Ballade of Dead Ladies," a translation of a poem by François Villon:

But where are the snows of yester-year?

and Mark Twain's *Roughing It:*

... the early gold mining was done ... you will find it hard to believe that there stood at one time a fiercely-flourishing little city ... the strangest population, the finest population, the most gallant host that ever tramped down the startled solitudes of an unpeopled land. And where are they now? ... *now* nothing is left of it all but a lifeless, homeless solitude. ... It is pitiful to think upon.

In the **carpe diem** motif, the speaker argues that life is short, time fleeting and therefore that life should be lived in the present, seized now, today, before it passes away: "Eat, drink, and be merry, for tomorrow we shall die." See "To His Coy Mistress," page 97. See also **CONVENTION, ARCHETYPE, STOCK CHARACTERS,** and **LEITMOTIF.**

MULTIPLE PLOT, more than one plot within a single work. For the sake of emphasis, an author may create more than one story with different sets of characters associated with each, making action, characters, and motives parallel or antithetical within the unity of the total work. For a discussion and example, see pp. 17-18.

NARRATIVE, in its broadest sense, a story—an account of an event or events by a speaker. A myth, folktale, epic, romance, allegory, satire, ballad, or novel is a narrative if there is both a story and a storyteller. For example, "Frankie and Johnny" (pp. 14-17), a narrative poem, is a tale in verse.

NOVEL, generally speaking, a fictitious narrative of considerable length. More than any other literary genre, the novel in its scope and form defies categorization. A novel may be long and panoramic, encompassing various elements of society, as does Leo Tolstoy's *War and Peace* (pp. 35-37), or may reflect one small segment of society, as does Jane Austen's *Pride and Prejudice* (p. 9). Though almost all novels are prose, the basis of Vladimir Nabokov's *Pale Fire* is in the form of a poem "in heroic couplets, of nine hundred ninety-nine lines, divided into four cantos." And one of the objects of a novel like John Barth's *Giles Goat-Boy* is to experiment with the form, style, and content of the novel itself, making it a still more elastic genre. The most that can be said of all novels, perhaps, is that they present an imaginative experience of life.

One way of distinguishing "kinds" of novels is according to the different aspects of experience they emphasize. The **PICARESQUE NOVEL** deals with a series of episodes out of the life of a person who is usually of low social level, a coarse, roguish fellow who makes his way in the world by using his wits to exploit the weaknesses and pretentions of people in various social classes. The **CHARACTER NOVEL** focuses on the protagonist's motives, his mental and emotional development, rather than on action, setting, or social conditions. A **BILDUNGSROMAN** refers to a character novel that deals with the "education," the growing up, of a young man. A **KUNSTLERROMAN** is concerned with the "education" of a young man as artist—the consciousness of the protagonist as he discovers his calling as writer, painter, musician. The **NOVEL OF MANNERS** portrays the social customs and conventions of a particular social class. It is closely linked with the **REGIONAL NOVEL,** which emphasizes a particular setting and shows the effect of that setting on the people living in it—their values, habits, emotional-mental outlook on life. In the **NOVEL OF IDEAS** the author is concerned primarily with the expression of a philosophical or cultural idea. The authors of the **"NEW NOVEL,"** a recent innovation, attempt to narrate experience without using plot, characterization, or setting—at least not in the same way previous novelists have used them.

These are but a few of many different "kinds" of novels, and the distinctions between them, of course, cannot be drawn sharply.

ODE, a long lyric poem dealing with one theme, written for a special purpose, usually praising or celebrating someone or something. Its stanzaic structure is often elaborate or irregular.

OMNISCIENT POINT OF VIEW. See Chapter 4, **POINT OF VIEW,** pp. 35-37.

ONOMATOPOEIA, the formation of a word so that its sound is associated with its meaning. For examples see pp. 47-48.

OTTAVA RIMA, a stanza of eight lines rhyming *abababcc,* usually written in iambic pentameter.

OVERSTATEMENT, a comparison which uses extravagant exaggeration for a deliberate effect. For examples see p. 69.

OXYMORON, a figure of speech which combines words with contradictory meanings or fuses apparently antithetical feelings or concepts. In Shakespeare's *Romeo and Juliet,* when the love-sick Romeo, in love with love, hears once again of the fighting in the streets between the Capulets and the Montagues, he speaks in oxymorons, "O brawling love! O loving hate! . . . O heavy lightness! serious vanity! . . . Feather of lead, bright smoke, cold fire, sick health! Still-waking sleep. . . ." See **PARADOX.**

PARADOX, a statement which at first appearance seems contradictory, absurd, or impossible but upon closer examination turns out to be true in some sense. The modern critic Cleanth Brooks has called poetry "the language of paradox," opposing it to science, "a language purged of every trace of paradox." The poet's method is to speak with intentional "indirection," expressing simultaneously contradictory ideas or qualities. It is a paradox that Shakespeare writes in "The Phoenix and the Turtle": "Love hath reason, reason none." It is a paradox that Lear (see pp. 2-3) is at once a kingly, great-hearted man and a narrow, peevish fool.

PERSONA, the mask, the "created-self" through whom the author speaks. In *Heart of Darkness* (see pp. 41-43), for example, Joseph Conrad, the author, does not speak in his own voice but creates a character, Marlow, who has personal qualities and distinctive attitudes toward both his audience and his subject. Conrad puts on his Marlow mask, so to speak, and it is the voice of this mask that we, the readers, hear telling the story.

Sometimes an author may seem to step forward in full person and tell his own story. But usually this is not as it seems. In *Roughing It* the author, Samuel Langhorne Clemens, may seem to be the speaker. But the "voice" we hear narrating the adventures is, consistently, one person with definite qualities and attitudes, an "imaginative projection" of Samuel Clemens, a youthful, naive, tenderfoot, a "turnip." Here is the "persona" describing his first horseback ride:

> I had quickly learned to tell a horse from a cow, and was full of anxiety to learn more . . . I brought the creature into the plaza, and certain citizens held him by the head, and others by the tail, while I mounted him. As soon as they let go, he placed all his feet in a bunch together, lowered his back, and then suddenly arched it upward, and shot me straight into the air a matter of three or four feet!

This is not Samuel Clemens speaking, not even the irascible Mark Twain, but an "eccentric creation of Mr. Clemens'," the persona of *Roughing It.* See **VOICE.** See also Chapter 6, **TONE,** p. 57; Chapter 4, **POINT OF VIEW,** p. 34.

PERSONIFICATION, a comparison that attributes human characteristics to inanimate objects. See p. 69 for examples.

PLOT. See Chapter 2, pp. 14ff.

POINT OF VIEW. See Chapter 4, pp. 34ff.

POETRY, most simply stated, words arranged in verse. But it is not the simple arrangement of words that makes poetry. If poetry is, as Emily Dickinson said, "what takes the top of your head off," then it must be extraordinary language, language raised to another level by its power, beauty, and dignity. Samuel Taylor Coleridge described poetry as, "the best words in the best order." Poetry, it has often been said, cannot be defined, only described. Rhythmical, concrete, compact, imaginative, and intense are some of the words used to distinguish poetry from prose. See **PROSE, VERSE.**

PROSE, in its most general sense, ". . . whatever is not verse is prose," as the philosophy master in Moliere's *The Bourgeois Gentleman* says. Though this definition is true in one sense, more may be said. Prose is the ordinary way we speak and write, that is, without rhyme or meter. And while there can be rhythm in prose writing, the rhythm is not regular or sustained. The absence of rhyme, meter, or regular rhythm does not imply that writing prose is less an art than writing poetry. The word prose also implies writing in which there is order through grammar and coherence, and style through diction and syntax.

PROSODY, an inclusive term meaning the principles or art of versification. See **METER, RHYTHM, STANZA.**

PROTAGONIST, the main character in a literary work, usually the hero. The protagonist is opposed by forces outside himself (for example, fate or nature), some aspect of himself (cowardice or anger), or more usually another person (the antagonist).

PUN, the humorous use of a word which is similar in sound to another word with a different meaning. For examples, see p. 48.

QUATRAIN, a stanza of four lines, sometimes rhymed, sometimes not. The **heroic quatrain** is written in an abab rhyme scheme in iambic pentameter.

RAISONNEUR, a character through whom the author speaks. In drama where he cannot enter and make comments, an author will sometimes create a character to come on stage and make comments for him. In Ibsen's "The Wild Duck," when Relling, the haughty, disillusioned, but gentle doctor, says, "Rob the average man of his life-illusion, and you rob him of his happiness at the same stroke," the reader feels that Ibsen is speaking through him, giving important clues to the meaning of the play. The raisonneur is not, of course, the author. An author may communicate his ideas through a character who is in many respects very different from himself.

RECOGNITION, that moment when a character sees the true condition of his existence. See p. 16.

RHYME, in verse, the repetition of sounds which are identical or similar. If the rhyming words are identical in sound except for their opening consonants, they make what is called a **perfect** rhyme, sometimes termed **true** or **complete.** Rhymes that are not exact are called **imperfect,** sometimes **near, half,** or **slant.** *Dust/must* is a perfect rhyme; *birch/march* an imperfect one.

Rhymes are classified according to (1) the number of rhymed syllables and (2) the position of the rhyming words in the line.

In a **single rhyme** only the final syllable is accented. Such a rhyme is also labeled **masculine** because it is vigorous and forceful as in *right/fight*. In a **double rhyme** both the last two pronounced syllables of the word rhyme with both the last two pronounced syllables of another word. This type of rhyme is also termed **feminine** since such rhymes are usually light and delicate as in *flower/power*. In **triple rhyme** the sound of the last three consecutive syllables of a word all correspond to the last three consecutive syllables of another word as in *precocious/atrocious*. Triple rhymes are rare and often produce a humorous effect.

Rhymes placed at the end of a line are called **terminal** or **end** rhymes as in the following lines from a poem by Walter Savage Landor:
   Yes; I write verses now and then,
   But blunt and flaccid is my pen,
   No longer talked of by young men.
When the rhyme occurs within a line it is called an **internal** rhyme. One of the rhyming words is usually the last word of the line as in this line from Coleridge's "The Rime of the Ancient Mariner":
   This Hermit good lives in that wood.
Rhyme is not essential to poetry. If rhyme is used effectively, however, it can enhance both the meaning and the feeling of a poem.

RHYME SCHEME, the pattern of rhymes in a poem. Letters of the alphabet are used to indicate rhyming lines. The letter *a* is assigned to the first line that is rhymed with another line. All other lines rhyming with this line are assigned the letter *a*. The second rhyme is labeled *b* and so on. The letter *x* is used for unrhymed lines. Following is an example of the rhyme scheme in Edmund Spenser's *The Fairie Queene*:

exceed	a
clawes	b
deed	a
pawes	b
drawes	b
tell	c
jawes	b
hell	c
fell	c

RHYTHM, the rate of movement of a sequence of words reflecting the activity of the author's thought and emotion. In English poetry, rhythm is usually communicated by a fairly regular pattern of stressed or unstressed syllables as in this line from Algernon Swinburne's "Atalanta,"
   From leaf to flower and flower to fruit.
See **METER**.

In prose, rhythm usually does not fall into a regular pattern but may show a definite cadence, a loose, informal rhythm, as in the following sentences from Walter Savage Landor's *Aesop and Rhodopé*:
   Laodameia died; Helen died; Leda, the beloved of Jupiter, went before. It is better to repose in the earth betimes than to sit up late; better, than to cling pertinaciously to what we feel crumbling under us, and to protract an inevitable fall.

In poetry the rhythm may be looked for in the syllables, in the metrical feet; in prose, rhythm exists in the longer units of phrase, sentence, and paragraph. In both poetry and prose, rhythm grows out of the pressure of the author's desire to express his thought and emotion.

RIME ROYAL, a stanza of seven lines of iambic pentameter, rhyming ababbcc.

RISING ACTION, that part of the action of a plot beginning with the exciting force and concluding with the climax. See pp. 16-17.

ROUND CHARACTER. See Chapter 1, **CHARACTER,** pp. 2-3.

SATIRE, the literary art of using ridicule as a device to expose and attack human vices, frailties, or institutions with the aim of correcting them. Both satire and comedy may evoke laughter, but comedy seeks to amuse, satire to deride. Either a passage in a work or the whole work may be termed satiric. When the object of the total work is satiric, then the work is a "satire" and is a literary genre, like tragedy or comedy. Most often, however, satire cuts across genre lines.

Critics sometimes divide satire into **direct** and **indirect.** In **direct satire** the object of ridicule is made clear by the speaker's direct reference to it. In *The Praise of Folly* Desiderius Erasmus created a speaker, a **persona,** Folly, who addresses her audience directly and who ridicules directly the "wise man":

> Put up against a fool some model of wisdom, one who lost his boyhood and youth in the classroom, who dissipated the best part of his life in continual worry and study, and who never tasted a particle of pleasure thereafter. He is always abstemious, poor, unhappy, and crabbed; ... pale, emaciated, sickly, sore-eyed, prematurely old and white-haired, dying before his time. Of course it really makes little difference when such a man dies. He never lived. Well, there is your wise man for you.

In **indirect satire** the object of ridicule is not formally named and addressed by a first person speaker but is perceived by the reader or audience to be the characters themselves—their opinions, vices, errors. In *Arms and the Man* George Bernard Shaw creates characters who are animated illustrations of the romantic opinions he ridicules (see Sergius's speech on p. 95).

SETTING. See Chapter 3, pp. 24ff.

SIMILE, a figure of speech in which the comparison between two things is directly expressed. For an example, see p. 68.

SITUATIONAL IRONY. See **IRONY.**

SOLILOQUY, a speech given by a character when he is alone, revealing his private thoughts and emotions. For a discussion and an example see p. 6.

SONNET, usually a poem of fourteen lines written in iambic pentameter expressing the poet's personal thought and emotion. Sonnets follow a definite rhyme scheme. The two most common types of sonnets are the **Italian or Petrarchan** and the **English or Shakespearian.**

The **Italian sonnet** consists of an octave (eight lines) rhyming abba abba, and a sestet (six lines) rhyming in various ways, commonly cde cde. Thought and rhyme often correspond: the octave may state a generalization, present a problem, raise a question, or describe a process (sunrise, for example); the sestet may give a specific example of the generalization, solve or ease the problem, answer the question, relate the process to the poet's own life.

The **English sonnet** is usually made up of three quatrains and a couplet commonly rhyming abab cdcd efef gg. Each quatrain may present concrete examples of an abstract idea, and the couplet may then draw a conclusion about them.

Another conventional sonnet form is the **Spenserian sonnet.** A blend of the Italian and English sonnets, its rhyme scheme interlocks or overlaps, abab bcbc cdcd ee. Here again variations in thought often correspond with rhyme scheme.

SPENSERIAN STANZA, a stanza of nine lines, eight lines of iambic pentameter followed by one line of iambic hexameter. The rhyme scheme is ababbcbcc.

SPONDEE. See **METER.**

STANZA, a group of two or more lines forming a division of a poem. Each stanzaic unit usually maintains a similar rhyme scheme, length, and predominant meter. In some poetry, stanzas do not follow a conventional form or regular pattern. Sometimes thought and meaning determine the stanzaic divisions called a *verse paragraph,* especially in **Blank Verse** or **Free Verse.** For specific conventional stanza patterns, see **Couplet, Tercet, Quatrain, Ottava Rima, Rime Royal, Spenserian Stanza.**

STOCK CHARACTER, a flat character who has become conventional. Like flat characters, stock characters have only one side to them. But unlike flat characters such as Bounderby or Pangloss (see pp. 1-2, 3-4), the stock character fits a conventional pattern. For example, when a character with hayseed in his hair comes on stage and alternately grins and gapes, we recognize the country bumpkin, the dimwitted rustic. We know just what to expect from this character, for we have seen the same type in other plays. A stock character, then, is a character type that recurs so frequently in literature that be becomes stereotyped: the sinister villain; the brave hero; the clever servant; the braggart soldier; the windy politician; the long-suffering, faithful woman; the irresistible, seductive female.

STREAM OF CONSCIOUSNESS, a literary technique in which the author records what goes on in the mind of a character. A character's thought is given as it occurs; his associative, random, fragmentary thinking shows the reader not only what the character thinks but the way his mind works as he thinks it. For a discussion and example, see pp. 40-41.

STRUCTURE. See Chapter 9, pp. 93ff.

STYLE. See Chapter 5, pp. 45ff.

SYNECDOCHE, a special kind of metaphor in which the part stands for the whole. For an example see p. 71.

SYMBOL. See Chapter 8, pp. 79ff.

SYNTAX, the arrangement or management of words to show the way they are hooked together as a unit, the way they relate to each other within a phrase or sentence. For a discussion of syntax, see pp. 45-51ff. For examples, see pp. 51-55.

TECHNIQUE, the various ways a writer handles his experience to produce a literary work; and, as used in this book, a term that refers to the various ways a reader has of discovering the writer's techniques.

In *Technique as Discovery* Mark Schorer has said that technique is the difference between experience and art:

> Everything is technique which is not the lump of experience itself, and one cannot properly say that a writer has no technique or that he eschews technique, for, being a writer, he cannot do so. . . . When we speak of technique, then, we speak of nearly everything. For technique is the means by which the writer's experience, which is his subject matter, compels him to attend to it; technique is the only means he has of discovering, exploring, developing his subject, of conveying its meaning, and, finally, of evaluating it.

Attention to technique is, as modern criticism has shown, a direct and objective means of focusing on a poem, play, or story for a better understanding of it, for a penetrating way of discovering it as a complex unity.

TENOR and VEHICLE, terms introduced by the critic I. A. Richards to refer to the two necessary elements of any metaphor: (1) the subject or thing being talked about, (2) the figure or metaphorical word which illustrates or explains the subject. When Hamlet says, "What should such fellows as I do crawling between earth and heaven?" there is a reference, Richards points out, to "other things that crawl." *Hamlet,* then, is the *tenor,* and the reference to other crawling things, the *vehicle.* Different kinds of words may be used metaphorically. In Richards' example the verbal "crawling" is metaphorical.

In the metaphor given on p. 69 of this book the metaphorical words are adjectives: "We are the hollow men/ We are the stuffed men." The *tenor* in this comparison is "We" and suggests, perhaps, twentieth century man. The *vehicle* is implicit in the adjectives "hollow" and "stuffed." In these words there is a reference to other things that are hollow and stuffed, "headpiece filled with straw."

If there are not two elements in a statement, if there are not both a tenor and a vehicle, then there is no metaphor. When there is both a tenor and a vehicle, it is the reader's task to determine what features or qualities the author implies they have in common. See **FIGURATIVE IMAGERY,** pp. 67 ff.

TERCET, a stanza of three lines usually with one rhyme.

TERZA RIMA, a poem composed of tercets. The rhyme scheme is aba bcb cdc dcd.

THEME, according to one definition, the "meaning," the view of life, embodied in the complex interrelation of all the various elements that shape and unify the total work. According to another definition, theme is the abstract subject of a work. For a discussion and examples, see pp. 105ff.

THESIS STATEMENT, the proposition a reader may advance about the "theme" of a work; the controlling idea of a critical paper. For a discussion, see pp. 105ff.

THIRD-PERSON POINT OF VIEW. See Chapter 4, **POINT OF VIEW,** pp. 34ff.

TONE. See Chapter 6, pp. 57ff.

TOPIC, as a specific subject for a critical paper on a literary work. See pp. 106ff.

TRAGEDY, commonly thought of as a story with an unhappy ending, in Greek drama, and conventionally ever since, represented by a mask with the corners of the mouth turned down. Such a definition, however, tells us little about this complex literary form. Here are some aspects of classical tragedy suggested by Aristotle's description of it: (1) a tragedy is concerned with an important and serious action; (2) the action is complete and unified, having a beginning, a middle, and an end; the conclusion is the logical outcome of the events that have preceded it; (3) the action is governed by a reversal in the protagonist's situation; (4) the protagonist suffers profoundly because of the reversal, and through this suffering recognizes things that he did not know before; in this way he achieves a higher degree of self-knowledge and, perhaps, a larger acceptance of life; (5) the total drama arouses in the spectator (who suffers with the tragic hero) emotions of pity and fear so as to effect a catharsis—a purgation or purification of these emotions.

Since Aristotle's time tragedy has changed. The most apparent change, perhaps, has been in the rank and social position of the protagonist. The heroes of ancient Greek tragedy and of most tragedy written before the late seventeenth century are not ordinary men, but kings or princes, extraordinary men who perform large passionate acts and who fall from high position to low. Arising from their unusual force and nobility, there is within these classical heroes a disposition to "excess"—to overweening pride or unbridled anger, to some aspect of self-will which gives rise to errors resulting in unbalanced actions. During the eighteenth century a kind of drama became popular in which the protagonists were not of high social position. The main characters of **bourgeois** or **domestic tragedy** are not extraordinary but "ordinary" middle class people, living "common" lives and speaking "common" words. In this century the protagonists of most dramas are from either the middle or the lower classes. The main character of a modern play may be a salesman, businessman, or housewife; a servant, prostitute, or laborer.

Critics sometimes distinguish differences in tragedies, not according to the social status of the protagonist but in respect to the nature of the forces that cause his downfall. When the cause of the downfall or misery of the protagonist is internal, arising primarily from a "fault" not "in our stars,/But in ourselves," the tragedy may be termed *"psychological."* When the fault is in the manmade world, in the cultural or economic world the protagonist lives in, the tragedy may be termed *"sociological."* When the fault lies in the very nature of human existence itself, and not so much in the man or in social forces but in the "stars," then the tragedy is termed *"cosmic."* Almost all tragedy is a blend of these three different kinds—only emphasis distinguishes them.

To some critics the most distinctive feature of tragedy is not so much the cause of the protagonist's misfortune as his response to it. In classical tragedy a protagonist of high stature fronts the catastrophe with a courage and nobility that reveal the greatness of the human spirit. And in many modern tragedies the protagonist faces defeat with spirit and dignity. If the main character dissolves in self-pity, however, or moral and psychological paralysis, a spiritless, puny victim of overwhelming forces of which he is completely unaware—then, even though the play is serious and ends unhappily, it is, according to some critics, more pathetic than tragic.

TROCHEE. See **METER.**

TROPE, the figurative use of a word. Trope means a "turn" from a word's literal meaning. The term is sometimes used to mean **FIGURE OF SPEECH.** See **FIGURATIVE IMAGERY,** pp. 67ff.

UNDERSTATEMENT, a figure of speech in which a writer creates a deliberate effect by saying less than he actually means. For an example see p. 70. See also **LITOTES** and **MEIOSIS.**

VEHICLE. See **TENOR.**

VERBAL IRONY. See **IRONY,** also pp. 60-61.

VERSE, a term meaning: (1) a single line of poetry; (2) any metrical composition, especially one light or trivial that is merely metered and rhymed but not on the artistic level of poetry. See **POETRY.**

VOICE, a term reserved by some critics to mean, not the "voice" of the speaker or the "voice" of the first-person narrator, but the "voice" of the creator of the total work, the unseen, pervasive presence that stands behind the work. See **PERSONA,** also Chapter 6, **TONE,** p. 57.

Index

abstract:
   meaning, 79-80, 82, 84, 88
   statement, 29-31, 65
   subject, 16, 105
abstract idea:
   and structure, 94, 97, 104
   and symbolism, 83, 87, 89-92
   and theme, 106
action, 17, 22-23, 92
   in allegory, 88
   and character, 7-8, 16
   and setting, 24-25, 31
   and symbol, 84-86
Adventures of Huckleberry Finn, The,
   first person point-of-view in, 39-40
Adventures of Robinson Crusoe, The,
   example of a loose sentence in, 49
Aeschylus, *Agamemnon,* 63
Agamemnon, dramatic irony in, 63
Alexandria Quartet, The, setting as it influences character, 25-26
allegory, 87-88
"Allegory of the Cave, The," as an example of allegory, 87
alliteration, 47, 56
analysis, 53, 68
anapest, 116
anti-plot, modern, 18, 21-23
antithesis, 18, 50-51
archetype, 116
Aristotle, on tragedy, 128-129
Arms and the Man, thematic structure of, 94-97
Arnold, Matthew, "Dover Beach," 73
assonance, 47-48, 56
attitude:
   author's, 58-59, 62, 65
   speaker's, 57, 60
Austen, Jane, *Pride and Prejudice,* 9
author:
   attitude of, 58-59, 62, 65
   and character, 4-5, 13
   and point of view, 34-41
   and subject, 59-60
   and tone, 58, 62

background, setting as, 27-28
balanced sentence, 49-51, 55-56
ballad, 116
Balzac, Honoré de, *Père Goriot,* 29-31
"Beast in the Jungle, The," structure of, 100-103

Beowulf, use of understatement in, 70
blank verse, 116
Bleak House, use of word as symbol in, 82-83
"Bliss":
   point of view in, 37-39
   outlined for critical paper, 106-108
bourgeois tragedy, 128-129
Browning, Robert, "Caliban upon Setebos," 6-7
Bunyan, John, *The Pilgrim's Progress,* 88

"Caliban Upon Setebos," as example of dramatic monologue, 6-7
Canterbury Tales, The:
   style of, 45-46
   tone in, 58-59
Candide, Pangloss as flat character, 3-4
"Canonization, The," example of overstatement in, 69
carpe diem, 121-122
Cary, Joyce, *The Horse's Mouth,* 26-27
catastrophe (*see* denouement)
central idea, 3, 89
character, 1-13, 77, 92
   actions as reflection of, 7-8
   in allegory, 87-88
   another character's comments about, 5
   author's comments about, 4-5
   author's relation to, 4-5, 13
   change in outlook of, 19
   comments on himself, 5-7
   complex, 4
   definition of, 1
   and events, 3
   flat, 1, 3-4, 13
   marking for, 9
   novel, 122
   and point of view, 34-41
   questions to ask about, 8, 13
   round, 2-4, 13
   and setting, 25-27
   simple, 4
   suggestions for writing about, 12-13
   and tone, 58, 60, 63
characteristic(s):
   diagramming one dominant, 10-12
   listing one character's, 9-10
characterization, methods of, 4-8

Index

Chaucer, Geoffrey, *The Canterbury Tales,* 45-46, 58-59
Chekhov, Anton, 18
   "In the Cart," 21-23
Clemens, Samuel L. (*see* Mark Twain)
climax, 16, 18, 22
"Collar, The," example of denotation and connotation, 47
closed couplet, 117
comedy, 117
   of manners, 117
comparison, 68-71, 77, 84
complication, 15, 17-18
conceit, 117
concrete, 79-80, 82, 87-89, 91-92
concrete details, 29-30, 105-106
conflict, 16-17, 22-23
connotation, 46-47, 56, 59
Conrad, Joseph, *Heart of Darkness,* 41-43, 58, 71-72
constructions:
   intense logical, 51-52
   unusual syntactical, 51, 53-55
controlling image (*see* image cluster)
convention, 117-118
couplet, 118
courtly love convention, 117-118
Crime and Punishment:
   character of Katerina, 4-5
   character of Marmelodov, 4-5
crisis, 16-17

dactyl, 118
Defoe, Daniel, *The Adventures of Robinson Crusoe,* 49
denotation, 46-47, 56
denouement, 16-17
describing, 64-65
diagramming:
   abstract correlations of setting, 31-33
   anti-plot, 21-23
   complex images, 70-72
   complex point of view, 41-43
   concrete details embodying abstract idea, 88-91
   cosmic irony, 62
   a dominant characteristic, 10-12
   dramatic irony, 63
   an event as symbol, 85
   a figure of speech as symbol, 84
   first person point of view, 40
   ironic elements, 66

diagramming (*continued*)
   metaphor, 69
   omniscient point of view, 36
   overstatement, 69
   plot of gradual change, 21
   sentences, 50-51, 54
   simile, 68
   situational irony, 62
   stream of consciousness, 41
   symbolic meaning, 79
   third-person-limited point-of-view, 39
   total action as symbol, 87
   understatement, 70
   verbal irony, 61
   word as symbol, 83
dialogue, 5-6, 118
Dickens, Charles:
   Bleak House, 82-83
   David Copperfield, 19
   Hard Times, 1-3
Dickey, James, "The Fiend," 80-82
diction, 46-48, 59, 64-65
disjunction, 52
domestic tragedy, 128-129
Donne, John:
   "The Canonization," 69
   "A Valediction: Forbidding Mourning," 75-77
Dostoyevsky, Fyodor:
   Crime and Punishment, 4-5
   The Possessed, 80, 82
"Dover Beach":
   imagery in, 73
   drawing, 73
drama, 118
   classical, 17
dramatic monologue, 6-7
dramatic structure, 118
drawing images, 72-73
Durrell, Lawrence, *The Alexandria Quartet,* 25-26

elegy, 118-119
Eliot, T. S.:
   "The Hollow Men," 69
   "The Love Song of J. Alfred Prufrock," 71
   The Waste Land, 58-59
Ellison, Ralph, *The Invisible Man,* 61-62
emotion and symbol, 82-83
emphasis, 80-82

English sonnet, 126
epic, 119
epic poem, 17, 119
essay, 119
Essay on Man, An:
   antithesis and parallelism in, 50
   an example of balanced sentence in, 51
Euripides, *The Trojan Women,* 27-28
events:
   plot, 14-15
   reasons for, 16, 19
   relationship of, 23
   and symbol, 82, 84-85, 92
exciting force, 16-17
exposition, 15-17

falling action, 16-17
Farewell to Arms, A, symbol in, 81-82
Faulkner, William, "A Rose for Emily," 31-32, 64-65
Faust:
   figure of speech used as a symbol, 83-84
"Fiend, The," use of emphasis in, 80-82
figure of speech, 68-70, 78
   as a symbol, 83-84, 92
Finnegans Wake:
   alliteration in, 47, 56
   assonance in, 47-48, 56
   onomatopoeia in, 47-48, 56
   pun in, 47-48, 56
first person point of view, 35, 39-40
Flaubert, Gustave, 46
"Fly, The," 18
foreshadowing, 119
formal essay, 119
Forster, E. M., *Howards End,* 81-82
"Frankie and Johnny"
   elements of plot in, 14-17
free verse, 119

genre, 119
Goethe, Johann Wolfgang von, *Faust,* 83-84
Grey, Zane, *Tappan's Burro,* 5-6

Hamlet:
   disjunctive style in, 52-53
   intense logical construction in, 52
   verbal irony in, 60-61

Hard Times:
   Bounderby as a flat character in, 1-3
Hardy, Thomas, *Jude the Obscure,* 62
Hawthorne, Nathaniel, "Young Goodman Brown," 19-21
Heart of Darkness:
   complex image in, 71-72
   point of view of, 41-43
Hemingway, Ernest, 49
   Farewell to Arms, A, 81-82
   Sun Also Rises, The, 67-68
Herbert, George:
   "The Collar," 47
   "Virtue," 93-94
heroic couplet, 118
heroic quatrain, 124
high comedy, 117
high point, 16, 22
"Hollow Men, The," example of metaphor in, 69
Homer:
   The Iliad, 10-12
   The Odyssey, 24-25
"Hopalong Sits In," character of Hopalong in, 9-10
Horse's Mouth, The, setting as it reveals character, 26-27
Howards End, symbolism in, 81-82
"Hunger Artist, The," total action as symbol, 85-87
hyperbole (*see* overstatement)

iamb, 120-121
Ibsen, Henrik, *Peer Gynt,* 85
idea and symbol, 82-83
Iliad, The, character of Agamemnon in, 10-12
image:
   cluster, 75
   literal, 67-68, 74, 78
imagery, 67-68
   complex, 70-72
   definition of, 67
   drawing, 72, 73
   figurative, 67-68
   listing, 73-74
   marking, 75-77
   suggestions for writing about, 77-78
incident, 14
informal essay, 119
"In the Cart," as example of modern anti-plot, 21-23

introduction, 15, 17. (*Also, see* exposition)
Invisible Man, The, situational irony in, 61-62
irony, 60-64, 66, 120
   cosmic, 62-63
   dramatic, 63-64
   incongruous elements in, 66
   situational, 61-62
   verbal, 60-61
Italian sonnet, 126

James, Henry, 8, 100
   "The Beast in the Jungle," 100-103
   "The Middle Years," 5
   "The Real Thing," 49-50
Jones, LeRoi, "Look for You Yesterday, Here You Come Today," 68
Joyce, James:
   Finnegans Wake, 47-48
   on point of view, 35
   Ulysses, 18, 40-41
Jude the Obscure, cosmic irony in, 62
Justine, setting in, 25

Kafka, Franz, "The Hunger Artist," 85-87
Keats, John, "Ode to a Nightingale," 73-74
King Lear, William Shakespeare, 2-3
   Lear as a round character, 2-3
Kunstlerroman, 122

"Lake Isle of Innisfree":
   author's relation to subject in, 34
   and point of view in lyric, 34
"L'Allegro," use of personification in, 69
language, 45-46
leitmotif, 120
listing:
   connotations to discover tone, 59
   denotation and connotations, 47
   images, 74
   one character's characteristics, 9-10
literal images (*see* image, literal)
litotes, 70, 120
"Look for You Yesterday, Here You Come Today," example of simile in, 68
loose sentence, 49, 55-56
"Love Song of J. Alfred Prufrock, The":
   example of synecdoche in, 71

"Love Song of J. Alfred Prufrock, The" (*continued*)
   imagery in, 71
low comedy, 117
lyric, 34, 120

Mansfield, Katherine, 18
   "Bliss," 37-39, 106-108
   "The Fly," 18
marking:
   abstract statements and concrete details, 30
   anti-plot, 22
   different characters, 9
   emotional structure, 99
   for structure, 93
   images, 75-77
Marvell, Andrew, "To His Coy Mistress," 97-98
McTeague,
   symbolism in, 88-91
meaning, 46-47, 60. (*See also* symbolic meaning)
   explicit, 60
   ironic, 60-64
   and theme, 105-106
meiosis, 120
metaphor, 69, 71
meter, 120-121
metonymy, 64
Midsummer Night's Dream, A, William Shakespeare
   as example of multiple plot, 17-18
Milton, John, "L'Allegro," 69
motif, 121-122
Mulford, Clarence E., "Hopalong Sits In," 9-10
multiple plot, 17-18, 122

narrative, 122
narrative poem, 17
narrator, 37-39, 41-43
new novel, 122
Norris, Frank, *McTeague,* 88-91
novel, 122
   of ideas, 122
   of manners, 122

objectivity, author's degree of, 34-35
O'Connor, Flannery, "Revelation," 7-8
ode, 122-123

"Ode to a Nightingale," literal images in, 73-74
Odyssey, The, and setting as it influences action, 24-25
"Of This Time, of That Place," symbolism in, 79-80
omniscient point of view, 35-37, 44
onomatopoeia, 47-48, 56
ottava rima, 123
outlining:
    abstract statements and concrete details, 31-33
    the plot of gradual change, 19-20
    to prepare a critical paper, 107-108
    the relationship of parts, 100-103
    thematic structure, 96-97
overstatement, 69
oxymoron, 123

paradox, 123
parallelism, 50-51, 55
Peer Gynt, 85
Père Goriot, setting in, 29-31
periodic sentence, 49-50, 55-56
persona, 123
personification, 69
    in allegory, 88
Petrarchan convention, 117-118
picaresque novel, 122
Pilgrim's Progress, The, as example of allegory, 88
Plato, *The Republic,* 87
plot, 14-23
    anti-, 18, 21-23
    beginning, middle, end, 16
    definition of, 14
    elements of, 14-17
    in modern story, 18
    multiple, 17-18
    of no change (*see anti-plot*)
    outlining, 17, 19-20
    reading for, 19
    suggestions for writing about, 23
poetry, 124
point of view, 34-44. (*See also* omniscient, third-person-limited, first person, stream of consciousness)
    definition of, 34
    diagramming, 41-43
    suggestions for writing about, 44
Pope, Alexander, *An Essay on Man,* 50-51
Possessed, The, and use of symbolism, 80, 82

Pride and Prejudice, as an example for marking characters, 9
prose, 124
prosody, 124
protagonist, 124
psychological tragedy, 130
pun, 48, 56

quatrain, 124

raissoneur, 124
Real Thing, The, example of periodic sentence in, 49-50
recognition, 16
regional novel, 122
Republic, The, as an example of allegory, 87
resolution, 17
"Revelation," and action as it reveals character, 7-8
rhyme, 124-125
rhyme scheme, 125
rhythm, 125
Richard III, and soliloquy as it reveals character, 6
rime royal, 125
rising action, 16-17
romantic comedy, 117
"Rose for Emily, A":
    setting and theme, 31-33
    tone in, 64-65
Roth, Philip, 49

"Sailing to Byzantium," and setting as state of mind, 28-29
satire, 126
"Second Coming, The," emotional structure of, 98-100
sense, 74
    and imagery, 67
sentence, 45-46, 49, 51, 56
    balanced, 50-51, 56
    construction, 49
    diagramming, 50-51, 54
    form, 49
    function, 49
    loose, 49, 56
    periodic, 49, 56
    structure, 46
setting, 24-33
    as it affects character, 25-26
    in allegory, 87-88
    as background, 27-28

setting (*continued*)
  as it causes action, 24-25
  definition of, 24
  functions of, 24
  as it reveals character, 26-27
  as a state of mind, 28-29
  suggestions for writing about, 33
Shakespeare, William:
  Hamlet, 51-53, 60-61
  King Lear, 2-3
  Midsummer Night's Dream, A, 17-18
  Othello, 5
  and point of view in drama, 34
  Richard III, 6
  Tempest, The, 53-55
Shaw, George Bernard, *Arms and the Man*, 94-97
simile, 68, 126
situation and symbol, 82-83
situational irony, 61-62
social comedy, 117
sociological tragedy, 128-129
soliloquy, 6
sonnet, 126
sound, 46-48, 56, 59
Spenserian sonnet, 126
Spenserian stanza, 126
spondee, 127
stanza, 127
Stein, Gertrude, 49-50
stock character, 127
stream of consciousness, 40-41, 127
  and first person point of view, 40
structure, 93-104
  emotional, 98-100
  logical, 97-98
  psychological, 100-103
  suggestions for writing about, 103-104
  thematic, 94-97
style, 45-56, 77. (*See also* diction, syntax, sentence)
  definition of, 45
  reading for, 46
  suggestions for writing about, 55-56
subjectivity, author's degree of, 34
Sun Also Rises, The, and use of literal images, 67-68
symbol, 79-92
  and abstract idea, 88-91
  definition of, 79
  diagramming, 89-91

symbol (*continued*)
  discovering and interpreting, 82
  events as, 84-85
  figure of speech as, 83-84
  total action as, 85-87
  word as, 82-83
symbolic meanings, 79-80, 88, 92
symbolism, 79-92
  common errors in reading, 79-80
  and emphasis, 80-82
  suggestions for writing about, 91-92
synecdoche, 71
syntax, 46, 49-51, 53-55, 64, 127
synthesis, 14, 16, 18

"Tappan's Burro," and dialogue as it reveals character, 5-6
technique, (*see* describing, diagramming, drawing, listening, marking, outlining)
temperament, 59, 65
Tempest, The, unusual syntactical construction in, 53-55
tenor, 128
tercet, 128
terza rima, 128
Thackeray, William Makepeace, on point of view, 35
theme, 105-106
  definition of, 105
thesis, 105, 106
  statement, 105
third-person-limited point of view, 35, 37-39, 44
"To His Coy Mistress," logical structure of, 97-98
Tolstoy, Leo, *War and Peace*, 35-37
tone, 57-66, 77
  definition of, 57
  reading for, 59
  relation to diction, 59, 64-65
  suggestions for writing about, 65-66
topic, 106, 108
tragedy, 128-129
Trilling, Lionel, "Of This Time, of That Place," 79-80
trochee, 120-121
Trojan Women, The, use of setting as background, 27-28
trope, 129
Twain, Mark, *Adventures of Huckleberry Finn, The*, 39-40

ubi sunt, 121-122
Ulysses:
   action as it reveals character, 18
   example of stream of consciousness, 40-41
understatement, 70. (*See also* litotes, meiosis)
   technique of, 18

"Valediction: Forbidding Mourning, A," complex imagery in, 75-77
Vanity Fair, 35
vehicle, 120
verbal irony, 60-61
verse, 129
Virginian, The, tone in, 57-58
"Virtue," structure of, 93-94
voice, 129
Voltaire, François-Marie Arouet *Candide,* 3-4

War and Peace, omniscient point of view in, 35-37
Waste Land, The, tone of, 58-59
Wister, Owen, *The Virginian,* 57-58
word, 45-49, 51-52, 56, 57-59, 67, 79-80
   as symbol, 82-83
word choice, 46, 49, 56
Wordsworth, William, "The World Is Too Much with Us," 60
"World is Too Much with Us, The," explicit meaning in, 60

Yeats, William Butler:
   "Lake Isle of Innisfree," 34
   "Sailing to Byzantium," 28-29
   "The Second Coming," 98-100
"Young Goodman Brown," as an example of plot of gradual change, 19-21